Mission Accomplished

Things Politicians Wish They Hadn't Said

Matthew Parris & Phil Mason

BOOKS

First published in 1996 as *Read My Lips*
Updated, revised and expanded editions published in Great Britain in
2007 and 2008 by JR Books, 10 Greenland Street, London NW1 0ND
www.jrbooks.com

A catalogue record for this book is available from the British Library.

ISBN 978-1-906217-66-2

10 9 8 7 5 4 3 2 1

Typeset by SX Composing DTP, Rayleigh, Essex
Printed by CPI Bookmarque, Croydon, CR0 4TD

Matthew Parris was born in 1949 in Africa. After seven years as a Conservative MP, he quit to follow Brian Walden as presenter of LWT's *Weekend World*. After 13 years as parliamentary sketch-writer for *The Times*, and subsequently as a columnist and broadcaster, he has become infamous for his wit, bite and style, and regularly appears on television and radio. He writes and reviews for a wide variety of publications, and regularly in *The Spectator*. He is also author of *Inca-Kola*, about his travels in Peru; three selections of his collected writing, *So Far So Good, Look Behind You* and *I Couldn't Possibly Comment;* and *Great Parliamentary Scandals*. He edited *Scorn: With Added Vitriol*, an hilarious collection of invective, which was published by Penguin, and (also with Penguin) his autobiography, *Chance Witness*, and his account of the rescue of an historic house in the Pyrenees, *Castle in Spain*. Since 1990 he has won many awards as columnist, author and commentator.

Phil Mason was born in Harwich, Essex, in 1958. He is a graduate of the London School of Economics, where he specialised in international politics. He has been a full-time civil servant since 1984. Specializing for over 30 years in collecting stories of the bizarre from around the world, he has amassed one of the country's largest private collections of cuttings and books chronicling the weird and the strange. His first book, *Would You Believe It?*, drawing on this archive, was published in 1990. He has also authored *Nothing Good Will Ever Come of It*, a compilation of misplaced predictions by parliamentarians, and contributed to Matthew Parris' *Scorn*. He lives in Gillingham, Kent, with his wife Allison, and son Phillip, accompanied by two cats and two dogs.

Contents

To the late Mme de Gaulle who,
asked by the late Lady Dorothy Macmillan
what she was looking forward to most,
replied, though she did not mean to,
'a penis'.

Acknowledgements

The sources for *Mission Accomplished* are too numerous to list in full. Over a hundred reference works were used, in addition to a mountain of privately collected press cuttings and, increasingly, news and political websites. Among the most useful published sources have been:

The Listener 'Out Takes' (BBC, 1982-1990); *Newsweek 'Perspectives'* (inaug. 1989 to date); *The Book of Political Quotes*, ed. Jonathon Green (London, 1982); *Forked Tongues* by Graham Jones (London, 1984); *They Got It Wrong!* ed. David Milsted (London, 1995); *The Longman Guide to Political Quotations*, ed. Caroline Rathbone and Michael Stephenson (London, 1985); *Nothing Good Will Ever Come of It* by Phil Mason (London, 1993); *Facts and Fallacies* by Chris Morgan and David Langford (London, 1981); *Observer Sayings of the Seventies*, ed. Colin Cross (London, 1979); *Presidential Anecdotes* by Paul Boller (Oxford, 1981); *Presidential Campaigns* by Paul Boller (Oxford, 1984); *Quotemanship* by Paul Boller (Dallas, 1967); *The Appeasers* by Martin Gilbert and Richard Gott (London, 1963); *Britain and Germany between the Wars* by Martin Gilbert (London, 1964); *Tony Blair: New Britain — My Vision of a Young Country — Selected Speeches* (New Statesman Special, London, 1996); *The Blair Necessities*, ed. Iain Dale (London, 1997); *The Wit of Prince Philip*, ed. Peter Butler (London, 1965); *Political Quotations* by Lewis Eigen & Jonathan Siegel (London, 1994); *The Experts Speak* by Christopher Cerf & Victor Navasky (New York, 1998).

Excerpts from Hansard are Parliamentary copyright and are reproduced by permission.
We are grateful to Julian Glover for preparatory research; to Adrian McMenaman from the Labour Party's press office; to Thomas O'Malley and Malcolm Gouderham from the Conservative Research Department; and to many others who have suggested, or helped find, quotations. We continue to collect. Readers who know or encounter quotations which might adorn a future edition are invited to let us have them.

Introduction

Here we are again. The world has moved on a decade since the original edition of this book (called *Read My Lips*) was published, but our politicians' gift for uttering the unwise, the outrageous and the just plain silly seems to have endured with little sign of decline. 'They have learned nothing and have forgotten nothing' French statesman Talleyrand is said to have said in 1796 of the behaviour of aristocratic politicians seven years after the Revolution. We see it the same way. As documenters of the theme, we are of course truly thankful.

The Bush family genes have continued to wreak their havoc on language, meaning and political foresight. We take our title for this updated edition from the banner strung behind the second President Bush when he spoke on the aircraft carrier *Abraham Lincoln* in May 2003 to signify to the American people and the world the supposed end of major combat operations in Iraq, 42 days after the invasion of the country and three weeks after the capture of Baghdad. Nearly six years on, that war continues with the United States military having suffered more than 4,000 combat deaths – 97 per cent of them after the 'Mission Accomplished' speech – and Iraq losing tens of thousands of civilians dead from the strife that has followed the downfall of Saddam Hussein.

Iraq has yielded a major crop of material for our update, enough for it to have a chapter of its own. It has not only produced a plethora of misplaced forecasts, but also regrettable phrases. Bush's incitement of insurgents – 'My answer is, bring 'em on' – was repaid in spades. CIA Director George Tenet asserted that the grounds for invasion amounted to a 'slam-dunk' case. The backtracking was slow and pained. It wended its way from US Secretary of State Colin Powell making the case to the UN Security Council just before the invasion – 'My colleagues, every statement I make today is backed up by sources, solid sources. These are not assertions. What we're giving you are facts and conclusions based on solid intelligence' – to Bush's admission to reporters four years later that things had not worked out as planned – 'It's bad in Iraq. Does that help?' George Tenet was more forthcoming: 'Those were the two dumbest words I ever said.' Bush later reflected that 'I learned some lessons about expressing myself maybe in a little more sophisticated manner.'

At least there were admissions of error, albeit grudging and long after everyone else had seen the reality of events. And how could there not be in circumstances such as these? Does this mark a change in political behaviour from what we saw in the past?

The preface to the original edition asked whether we should harry politicians for simply changing their mind. Of course not. The point being made by many of the quotations in the collection was something different. It is not the act of changing one's mind, but the open acknowledgement that one's doing so that appears to be the hardest thing for politicians to concede. Tenet's reflection was refreshingly candid (but then in the circumstances, could he have done otherwise?)

Where politicians have more room for manoeuvre, few are so forward. How many times have we heard a politician say, 'Well, I now believe x to be the case; I accept I once said y, but things have changed, I've considered the evidence again and for me this points to x. I have no qualms in changing my mind. Nor should you, elector, have any qualms either in my doing so. It's responsible behaviour.' How grown-up that would be. But do we see it? Of course not. We get changes in mind, certainly, but you would hardly ever know that it's a change. Statements are forcefully uttered which are contrary to previous positions uttered with equal force, but no hint that the new stance in fact represents a shift of attitude. Or worse, the politician makes a deliberate attempt to lure listeners into believing that their current position represents a consistency of belief.

An illustration of the first kind is the seismic shift of Tony Blair on trade union reform which, in the 1980s, saw greater regulation to ensure unions balloted members before taking strike action. In 1983, his was a traditional left perspective: 'The extraordinary proposition [is] advanced that it is the proper role of the government to interfere in the due process of a voluntary organisation . . . It is thoroughly unconscionable and wrong to tell trade unions how to run elections.' When asked as Labour leader in 1995 whether he would keep the reforms, his reply was, 'Heavens above, that is common sense.' His choice of words, implying that no normal thinking person could ever have had any other view, masked to those listening then his own comprehensive reversal of position.

Paddy Ashdown's movement on nuclear defence is a classic example of the more devious approach. As a newly elected Liberal MP in 1984 he declared the nuclear deterrent to be 'A monstrous folly which we should divest ourselves of as soon as possible.' Fair enough. A clear political position. We can respect him for that. In the years that followed, his views changed – no problem there for anyone surely – but he couldn't bring himself to admit it. That's the problem. As party

Introduction

leader, just before the 1992 general election, he told the BBC, 'I never took the view that this country did not need an independent deterrent.' Had he changed his mind? Yes. Was he willing to acknowledge that to the public? No. That's the point. If it was not for fact-checkers going back into the record to dig out earlier statements, no one listening in 1992 would have reason to suspect that the leader of this major party had been anything other than a paragon of consistency in thought and perception.

Perhaps it is this consistency that we, electors, subconsciously look for in our leaders, and which they feel they need to reflect back to us. Subconsciously, because if we thought about it rationally, we ourselves rarely stay with the same views as both we as individuals and the world around us change constantly. But evidently politicians, who occupy the same changing world, and change themselves, feel it is too risky to mirror too explicitly the changing flux of opinion.

Take Chancellor of the Exchequer, Denis Healey, amidst the economic crisis of 1976. In April of that year, he was forecasting in his budget that 'By the end of next year, we shall be on our way to that so-called economic miracle we need.' In July, he was urging the British public to keep faith: 'If we can keep our heads – and our nerve – the long-awaited economic miracle is in our grasp.' By December, his view had evidently changed, but you wouldn't have known it if you had only listened to him then: 'What I have always said is that no government can produce an economic miracle.'

He could have admitted that his vision was unfulfilled. Instead, he felt it safer to deny he had had the view in the first place. It is this lack of confidence in acknowledging they are changing their mind, not the change itself, that is currently the form of our political game.

Some have taken a bolder stride towards confessing, but still feel the need to distance themselves from a simple human admission. When New Mexico Governor Bill Richardson was caught out with an inaccurate claim in his biographical details that he had once been recruited by the Kansas City A's, a major league baseball team, a claim he had maintained on his CV for four decades, he responded to the charge of deception with an equally audacious reply, issuing a press release stating, 'After being notified of the situation and after researching the matter . . . I came to the conclusion that I was not drafted by the A's.'

All this provokes cynicism and distrust in electors – but for the authors, we confess, much humour, and a good portion of this book.

But this category of verbal gymnastics is just one of many themes covered in this book. We have kept the same chapter themes, but most

Introduction

have been substantially revised with new material. New heroes emerge – George W Bush (the harvest is so substantial that we have had to be selective. We have consciously foregone quarrying the mountain of linguistic contortions which are available in other publications); Donald Rumsfeld, Boris Johnson, John Prescott, while other old favourites – Prince Philip, Ken Livingstone, Tony Blair – have more to their name.

The motivation of this edition remains as before: to entertain, poke fun, burst a few egos and perhaps provoke a little thought. But not too much. We don't take ourselves, or politicians, too seriously.

Admitting one got it wrong will, we predict, remain as difficult as it has always been. In 2007, Defence Secretary Des Browne offered a classic perambulation around the challenge, 'I have expressed a degree of regret that can be equated with an apology.' So long as the sense exists among politicians that it is a requirement of politics to equivocate, dissemble and sometimes simply deceive, there will always be new editions of the collection you are now about, we hope, to enjoy.

Phil Mason
Matthew Parris

1

Oops!

Simple Blunders

Need we say more . . . ?

Exchange between first ladies during visit by Harold Macmillan to Paris to mark General de Gaulle's retirement:

Dorothy Macmillan: What are you looking forward to now?
Madame de Gaulle: A penis.
General de Gaulle: My dear, I think the English don't pronounce the word quite like that. It's not 'a penis', but 'appiness'.

This is a great day for France.

RICHARD NIXON, in Paris for the funeral of President Pompidou, 1974

He made a great contribution to public life, especially in France.

JOHN MAJOR, speaking at the funeral of President Mitterrand, 1996

To His Majesty the King of Sweden!

JAMES CALLAGHAN, Foreign Secretary, proposing a toast to his host at a dinner in Oslo, Norway

[You are] a worthy representative of the new democracy in Brazil.

CALLAGHAN, Prime Minister, toasting General Ramalho Eanes, President of Portugal, at a summit meeting of leaders of NATO (of which Brazil is not a member), London, May 1977

Oops! Simple Blunders

It is marvellous to be in South Island.

THE DUKE OF DEVONSHIRE, Foreign Office minister in Macmillan's government, on arrival in North Island, New Zealand

I want to thank the Mayor of Rio for his warm welcome.

French President, JACQUES CHIRAC, arriving in Buenos Aires, Argentina, March 1997

You too have difficulties with unemployment in the United States.

MARGARET THATCHER – while visiting Canada, 1982

Either you act firmly against drug traffickers, or I close the borders.

JACQUES CHIRAC, French President, to Wim Kok, Dutch Prime Minister at a summit, 1995. (France and Holland do not share a border)

Norway and Portugal are on their own edge of Europe. You are placed on the Mediterranean's warm beaches, we are as far north as it is possible to be.

CROWN PRINCE HAAKON, mixing up geography in welcoming the Portuguese President on an official visit, February 2004. Portugal has an entirely Atlantic coastline. When the speech was posted on the internet, it had also mis-spelt Portugal's most famous footballing legend, Eusebio

How are you, Mr Mayor? I'm glad to meet you.

RONALD REAGAN failing to recognize his own Secretary for Housing and Urban Development, Samuel Pierce, at a White House reception for US mayors, 1981

To President Figueiredo and the people of Bolivia . . . I mean Brazil. Bolivia's where I'm going next.

REAGAN, toasting his host in Brasilia, 1982. (He was going to Colombia. Bolivia was not on the itinerary)

I would like to extend a warm welcome to Chairman Mo.

REAGAN, toasting Liberian President, Samuel Doe, 1982

Oops! Simple Blunders

Nice to see you again, Mr Ambassador.

REAGAN greeting (for the first time) Denis Healey, Labour's foreign affairs spokesman, visit to White House, 1987

What's in a name? I'm sorry.

MARY ROBINSON, Irish President, at a state banquet in Washington, apologizing to her host President Clinton whom she had called President Kennedy, June 1996

There's a cord sticking out of the back of my DVD machine. Might you tell me where it goes?

PRINCE PHILIP to actress Cate Blanchett upon being told that she worked in the entertainment industry, February 2008

It was an honour to welcome the distinguished Prime Minister of India.

US senator JESSE HELMS, chairman of the Senate foreign relations committee, briefing the press after a meeting with Benazir Bhutto, Prime Minister of Pakistan, 1995

Kim Jong the Second.

JESSE HELMS referring to North Korean leader Kim Jong Il, 1995

I take pride in the words, *Ich bin ein Berliner* [I am a doughnut].

President JOHN KENNEDY, at the Berlin Wall, June 1963. (What he meant to say – 'I am a Berliner' – should have been '*Ich bin Berliner*'. Adding the indefinite article '*ein*' turned it into a description of a traditional central European sticky bun)

On this beautiful Irish day, I feel like a real Dub. Is that what I'm supposed to say?

President BILL CLINTON, addressing an audience of Dubliners during his visit to Ireland, December 1995

I'm surprised because if you arrive in Windhoek, it doesn't seem like you're in an African country. Few cities of the world are so clean and beautiful as Windhoek.

Brazilian President LUIZ IGNACIO LULA, at a public ceremony on his departure from the Namibian capital during his four country Africa tour, November 2003

I sometimes feel like King Canute. Yes, indeed. Just like King Canute with his finger in the dyke.

NIRJ DEVA, Conservative MP, on battling EU bureaucracy, March 2001

The Minister for School Standards and myself [sic] meet regularly with those parent's [sic], teacher's [sic] and head's [sic] who have a commitment to raising standards.

Parliamentary written answer drafted by officials at the Department for Education and posted under the name of the Education Secretary, DAVID BLUNKETT, February 2001

That's fine phonetically, but you're missing just a little bit.

Vice-President DAN QUAYLE, adding an 'e' to 'potato' written by a sixth-grade pupil, Trenton, New Jersey, June 1992

Fifty-four.

STEPHEN BYERS, Schools Minister, asked to multiply eight by seven (56) during a BBC radio interview, January 1998. A No. 10 press spokesman, reaffirming the Prime Minister's confidence in him, said 'it is one of those character-forming events'. There was further controversy over Byers' skills for his ministerial duties when after the 2001 election, he was appointed Secretary of State for Transport despite not being able to drive a car

Can I have a pot of that nice avocado mousse?

PETER MANDELSON, reported remarks in a fish and chip shop in his Hartlepool constituency, pointing to the mushy peas. He insists the story is apocryphal

4

Oops! Simple Blunders

It must be all that sea air in Harrogate.

PATRICIA HEWITT, Secretary of State for Trade and Industry, House of Commons,
March 2002, cracking a joke at Conservative members who had just returned
from their annual spring conference in the town. Harrogate is about 50 miles
from the coast

Has it taken any pictures of the flag planted by Neil Armstrong?

US Congresswoman SHEILA JACKSON-LEE, a member of the House Space and
Aeronautics Committee, on a visit to the control centre of the Mars Pathfinder
mission, September 1997

Do you have blacks, too?

GEORGE W. BUSH, to Brazilian President Fernando Cardoso, June 2002.
Witnessed, but not reported, by the White House press corps. Brazil has the
largest population of blacks of any country outside Africa.

Errrr.

TOM HARKIN, Iowa Senator, mispronouncing America's top-rated hospital drama,
ER (which is pronounced as initials) during a healthcare reform speech, April
1998. He had asked his aides for a draft speech showing him to be 'in touch' with
the people. He had, in fact, never heard of the show

Thank you for your letter regarding the protection of the Texas
eagle. I share your view that the urgent problem of species
extinction and the conservation of biological diversity should be
addressed . . .

America's Vice-President AL GORE replying to letter from Dallas man complaining
about budget cutbacks which threatened a local train service called the Texas
Eagle, December 1996

This is Pearl Harbor Day. Forty-seven years ago to this very day,
we were hit and hit hard at Pearl Harbor.

GEORGE BUSH SNR, campaigning for the presidency, speaking to the American
Legion in Louisville, Kentucky, on 7 September 1988, three months before the
actual anniversary on 7 December

Is the West Bank a publicly or privately owned institution?

ENZO SCOTTI, short-serving Italian foreign minister – just 25 days – raising a query on a briefing paper on the Israeli-occupied territories, reported *The Times*, 1992

Wait a minute, I'm not interested in agriculture – I want the military stuff.

WILLIAM SCOTT, Virginia Senator in 1970s, interrupting a briefing from Pentagon officials when they began talking of (missile) silos

Do you like the work?

RICHARD NIXON, first words to a member of his police escort team lying injured in the road after an accident involving the Presidential motorcade, St Petersburg, Florida, 1970

Do you do stand-up?

CHERIE BLAIR, the Prime Minister's wife, greeting a wheelchair-bound comedian at the Labour Party conference, September 2005

I note the tremendous progress of this city. The Mayor was telling me in the last twelve years . . . you have had practically a doubling of population. Where has this progress come from? That progress has not come primarily from government, but it has come from the activities of hundreds of thousands of individual Mississippians . . .

RICHARD NIXON, campaigning in Mississippi, 1960

You certainly can't say that the people of Dallas haven't given you a nice welcome.

NELLIE CONNALLY, wife of John Connally, Governor of Texas, to President Kennedy on arrival in Dallas. He was assassinated hours later, November 1963

Oops! Simple Blunders

Hong Kong: Takes Your Breath Away.

Long-running advertising slogan of the HONG KONG TOURIST BOARD, which was withdrawn in April 2003 during the outbreak of the deadly SARS virus that killed over 300 people in the territory

Du Bist Deutschland.

'You are Germany', the slogan of a £20m German government campaign in 2005 to instil national pride, backfiring when historians discovered the same slogan had been used by the Nazi Party to promote Hitler's Germany in the 1930s

How did I know the B-1 bomber was an aeroplane? I thought it was vitamins for the troops.

RONALD REAGAN

My fellow Americans, yesterday the Polish government, a military dictatorship, a bunch of no-good lousy bums . . .

REAGAN, voice test for radio statement, inadvertently broadcast, 1981

My fellow Americans, I'm pleased to tell you today that I've signed legislation that will outlaw Russia forever. We begin bombing in five minutes.

REAGAN, radio microphone sound test inadvertently broadcast, 1984

I've talked to you on a number of occasions about the economic problems our nation faces, and I am prepared to tell you it's in a hell of a mess – we're not connected to the press room yet, are we?

REAGAN, voice test mistakenly broadcast to the press corps

She has indicated to [Mr Kinnock] that she would not be able to be here because she has made herself available to Mr Gorbachev.

Celebrated *double-entendre* explanation by JOHN WAKEHAM, Leader of the House, standing in for Margaret Thatcher at Prime Minister's Question Time during the visit to Britain by the Soviet leader, April 1989. (According to one account, it led to the longest sustained laughter in the Commons in memory)

For almost two years now we have tried to manage the economy in a way that no economy has been managed before.

GEORGE BROWN, Deputy Prime Minister, House of Commons, July 1966, unintended ambiguity on Labour's economic stewardship during a debate on crisis measures requiring a rise in interest rates, a wages' freeze and cuts in public expenditure and investment

How nice to see you all here.

ROY JENKINS, addressing prisoners on a visit to a London jail

I believe in calling a spade a spade.

ROY HATTERSLEY, Labour shadow home affairs spokesman, following a strident speech against racism, which prompted from the audience the question: 'Is it right to openly refer to race and racism?', August 1983

At Consett you have got one of the best steelworks in Europe. It doesn't employ as many people as it used to because it is so modern.

KENNETH CLARKE, Chancellor of the Exchequer, BBC Radio Newcastle, March 1995. The works had closed in 1980

I think [Consett] is also one of the major centres for disposable baby nappies as well.

CLARKE two weeks later; the nappy factory had closed in 1991

These people have closed down so much of British industry that they cannot be expected to remember all of it.

BRIAN WILSON, Labour shadow trade and industry spokesman, 1995

In the four years I have had the privilege of being your Member of Parliament . . .

Opening lines of letter from GYLES BRANDRETH, to the 2,000 inhabitants of the village of Saughall, Cheshire, assuring them he remained 'in touch' with his electors, November 1996. The village was in the neighbouring constituency

Oops! Simple Blunders

Dear Dr Meyer. You can provide us with an essential part of the Conservative election machine. A £20 donation goes straight towards communication to 4,000 people. . . . Of course, modern electioneering requires . . . targeted mailing.

Mailshot letter from BRIAN MAWHINNEY, Conservative Party Chairman, December 1996. Councillor Percy Meyer was chairman of the Liberal Democrats in Prime Minister John Major's Huntington constituency. Similar letters were received by, amongst others, Denis MacShane, Labour MP for Rotherham, and Lord Jenkins, former Social Democrat leader

And nowhere can we be more proud than here in [insert constituency name] . . .

Line included in mailshot sent by LIZ BLACKMAN, Labour MP for Erewash, to her constituents February 2005, which revealed the widespread practice among Labour members of using standard replies produced at Party Headquarters

Owing to the disillusionment of the House on Tuesday 8th April, we are endeavouring to clear all outstanding accounts.

Excerpt from letter sent to all MPs by the FINANCE OFFICE, House of Commons, about the dissolution of Parliament, March 1997

Our priority is to create jobs. This is not just an economic priority but also a social and moral one.

CONSERVATIVE MANIFESTO, 1997, page 9

Governments cannot create jobs.

CONSERVATIVE MANIFESTO, 1997, page 10

You can only be sure with the Conservatives.

CONSERVATIVE MANIFESTO, 1997, title

Slee's Hardwood Shop.

Shop sign JOHN MAJOR unwittingly allowed himself to be photographed against, Barnstaple, Devon, general election campaign, March 1997

Thirty injured, nobody dead. At the end of this opera everybody's dead.

Sɪʀ Pᴀᴛʀɪᴄᴋ Mᴀʏʜᴇᴡ, Northern Ireland Secretary, responding to journalists' questions on the latest IRA bomb attack, as he was arriving to see Donizetti's *Lucia di Lammermoor*

I'm quite deliberate sometimes about getting into the tabloid press and on TV because I think that if responsible politicians don't do it, then irresponsible ones will.

Eᴅᴡɪɴᴀ Cᴜʀʀɪᴇ, Conservative MP for South Derbyshire, 1983

Most of the egg production in this country sadly is now infected with salmonella.

Cᴜʀʀɪᴇ, junior health minister, on TV, 1988. The claim was described by the Egg Industry Council as 'factually incorrect and highly irresponsible'. She resigned a fortnight later.

People in the north die of ignorance and crisps.

Cᴜʀʀɪᴇ, two weeks after becoming a junior health minister, September 1986

Cervical cancer is the result of being far too sexually active – nuns don't get it.

Cᴜʀʀɪᴇ

Good Christian people . . . will not catch AIDS.

Cᴜʀʀɪᴇ, February 1987

Postpone that second holiday and use the money for an operation.

Cᴜʀʀɪᴇ, January 1988

Buy long Johns, check your hot-water bottles, knit gloves and scarves and get your grandchildren to give you a woolly night-cap.

Cᴜʀʀɪᴇ, advice to pensioners on dealing with winter cold

Don't have an affair.

Advice given in a 'Dad Pack' developed by the DEPARTMENT FOR EDUCATION AND SKILLS to help men become responsible fathers, June 2006

All you have to do [to protect yourself from radiation] is go down to the bottom of your swimming pool and hold your breath.

Spokesman for the US DEPARTMENT OF ENERGY, date unknown

If a competent and suitable woman was appointed to the British Railways Board, more attention would be paid to cleaning up the stations.

LADY WARD of North Tyneside, 1975

And in Frank Dobson's Camden, would you believe, they gave a grant to the Camden Hopscotch Asian Women's Group.

BRIAN MAWHINNEY, Conservative Party Chairman, annual conference, October 1995. The organization turned out to be a community project funded by the Home Office, with the Princess Royal as its patron. 'We picked an unfortunate example,' a party official said

As Secretary of State for Ireland . . .

PETER MANDELSON, Northern Ireland Secretary of State, in his opening words to the House of Commons after taking up his post in October 1999, appearing to solve the Irish Question at a stroke

Ah, I must have been reading it upside down. I thought it was 81, which did seem most unfair.

UNIDENTIFIED BISHOP in the House of Lords, asked if he would support the 18 compromise in the coming debate on the age of homosexual consent, 1994

Waste in any form is something that no council should accept.

ERNIE FLOOD, Mayor of Maidstone Borough Council, as he christened the council's new bottle bank by spraying a bottle of champagne over it, 1980

This skunk is unbelievably powerful. It's completely different to – I think I'll stop there.

Conservative leader, DAVID CAMERON, on drugs' control plans, July 2007

Through your work as journalists, you tell the world important stories which have to battle against gossip, trivia and celebrity for attention.

JOHN SENTAMU, Archbishop of York, addressing the One World Media Awards, which focus on media coverage of global development issues, June 2008, less than a week after becoming the first archbishop to do a charity parachute jump, a feat which, without difficulty, competed very successfully for widespread media coverage

After the war, France and England should join hands to make a formidable fart.

DUKE OF WINDSOR, addressing French troops during the Second World War. Speaking in French, he mistakenly used the masculine article which changed the meaning of his words

Those c**ts in Defence Medical Services have gone too far . . .

Slip of the tongue by JOHN SPELLAR, junior defence minister, answering questions in the House of Commons, January 2000. He had meant to refer to 'cuts' in services

If we're going to maintain America's status as the number one maritime power . . . it means having modern musicians and well-trained sailors.

MICHAEL DUKAKIS, Democratic candidate for US President, 1988. (He meant 'modern munitions')

It is a scandal that there are two and a half homeless people in America.

MICHAEL DUKAKIS, campaign 1988. (He meant two and a half million)

Oops! Simple Blunders

I am not wanting to make too long speech tonight as I am knowing your old English saying, 'Early to bed and up with the cock.'

HUNGARIAN DIPLOMAT, speech to an embassy reception

I asked the barmaid for a quickie. I was mortified when the man next to me said it's pronounced 'quiche'.

Italian Ambassador to Britain, LUIGI AMADUZZI, 2001

Thank you all very much for coming out today.

Idaho Senator LARRY CRAIG, starting his explanatory statement to the press in August 2007 having become embroiled in a sex scandal following his arrest for alleged lewd behaviour in a public toilet at Minneapolis airport. The statement was arranged for him to deny that he was gay

I cannot think what to say. So I will ask my two daughters to sing to you.

General election broadcast by the ECOLOGY PARTY in Poland, 1991

Yes, gradually.

MILTON OBOTE, President of Uganda, replying to question whether his programme of eliminating all vestiges of British colonial rule would include switching to driving on the right, 1971

It is white.

GEORGE W. BUSH, to a child who had asked what the White House was like, on visit to Britain, July 2001

Watch the borders!

Manuscript scrawl by FBI head J. EDGAR HOOVER on a memo to remind typists to leave wide margins (where he liked to scribble his comments). Misunderstanding, his deputy put bureau offices near Canada and Mexico on maximum alert for several weeks expecting an increase in illegal immigrants (attrib.)

Well, of course, the Prime Minister has been working very hard at it.

Foreign Secretary ROBIN COOK in response to effusive congratulations from Bertie Ahern, Irish Premier, November 1999. Cook assumed Ahern must be referring to a breakthrough he hadn't heard about in the Northern Ireland peace talks. He was, in fact, referring to news that Cherie Blair was pregnant, which Cook hadn't heard about either

Put a tail on me and see how bored you'll be.

Ill-fated challenge to the press by presidential hopeful GARY HART, 1987. They did, and quickly uncovered his extramarital relationship with model Donna Rice which abruptly scuppered his campaign

No socialist system can be established without a political police . . . they would have to fall back on some form of Gestapo.

WINSTON CHURCHILL, as Prime Minister, election broadcast against the Labour Party, 1945. The remark, widely deplored, seriously undermined his campaign. He lost

My, you must have fun chasing the soap round the bath.

PRINCESS DIANA, shaking hands with a one-armed man, Australian visit, 1983

We could go for marriage, an affair or casual sex.

PADDY ASHDOWN, Liberal Democrat leader to Prime Minister Tony Blair in the run-up to the 1997 general election about possible links between the two parties, revealed in Ashdown's memoirs in 2000

If Prime Minister Sharon had lived . . . he is dead, isn't he? [No?] It's an easy mistake to make.

KIM HOWELLS, Middle East Minister, giving evidence to the Foreign Affairs Select Committee, March 2007. Members had to enlighten him that Sharon still remained in the coma he had been in for over a year

Oops! Simple Blunders

What a load of old crap that was.

Jose Maria Aznar, Spanish Prime Minister, unaware his microphone was still on after giving a speech at an EU Summit in Barcelona, March 2002

I could not fail to disagree with you less.

Boris Johnson, *Have I Got News for You*, BBC TV, December 2003. It won the 2004 annual 'Foot in Mouth Award' from the Plain English Campaign

Like these lions I read about in Botswana that attack elephants for some reason.

Johnson on journalists, October 2006

The extreme reaction to Mr Bigley's murder is fed by the fact that he was a Liverpudlian. Liverpool is a handsome city with a tribal sense of community. A combination of economic misfortune . . . and an excessive predilection for welfarism have created a peculiar, and deeply unattractive, psyche among many Liverpudlians. They see themselves whenever possible as victims, and resent their victim status; yet at the same time they wallow in it. Part of this flawed psychological state is that they cannot accept that they might have made any contribution to their misfortunes, but seek rather to blame someone else for it, thereby deepening their sense of shared tribal grievance against the rest of society.

Johnson getting into trouble with the city of Liverpool, October 2004. Ken Bigley was a British contract worker who had been kidnapped by terrorists in Iraq and held for a month before being murdered

In our maturity as a civilization, we should accept that we can cut out the cancer of ignorant sentimentality without diminishing, as in this case, our utter disgust at a foul and barbaric act of murder.

Johnson's concluding sentence, overestimating the maturity of modern society.

Oops! Simple Blunders

I'm here to say sorry for the things I can apologize for in that editorial that you've been discussing. I obviously can't retract every word of it, and I wouldn't. It would be just madness if I came here and started saying that I disapproved one week of something I ordered in the previous week. And I do think the piece made valid points, and I stick by them.

JOHNSON, a week later, forced by the Conservative Party to visit Liverpool personally to apologize, October 2004

I am a squeezed lemon on this subject.

JOHNSON responding to reporters' requests for comment during his visit to Liverpool

There are far too many feral children running around [in Islington] because there are far too few police on our streets.

JOHNSON, when prospective Conservative candidate, fringe meeting, at the Conservative annual conference, October 2000

For 10 years we in the Tory Party have become used to Papua New Guinea-style orgies of cannibalism and chief-killing, and so it is with a happy amazement that we watch as the madness engulfs the Labour Party.

JOHNSON upsetting the Papua New Guinea government, September 2006

I would like to thank the High Commissioner very much for her clarification. I meant no insult to the people of Papua New Guinea who I'm sure lead lives of blameless bourgeois domesticity in common with the rest of us.

JOHNSON apologizing after the Papua New Guinean representative in London called the comment 'out of touch with the modern PNG'. He said he would be happy 'to add Papua New Guinea to my global itinerary of apology'

Here we are, in one of the most depressed towns in Southern England, a place that is arguably too full of drugs, obesity, underachievement and Labour MPs.

JOHNSON taking aim this time at Portsmouth, April 2007

The dreadful truth is that when people come to see their MP they have run out of better ideas.

JOHNSON, writing in the *Daily Telegraph*, September 2003

My chances of being PM are about as good as the chances of finding Elvis on Mars, or my being reincarnated as an olive.

JOHNSON, writing in the *Independent*, June 2004

Look the point is . . . er, what is the point? It is a tough job but somebody has got to do it.

JOHNSON, on being appointed shadow arts minister, May 2004

I'm making absolutely no comment . . . and no, I did not.

JOHNSON, when asked if he intentionally misled Michael Howard, leader of the Conservative Party, who sacked him for lying about an extramarital affair, December 2004

My friends, as I have discovered myself, there are no disasters, only opportunities. And, indeed, opportunities for fresh disasters.

JOHNSON, on being sacked as shadow arts minister, December 2004

Nothing excites compassion, in friend and foe alike, as much as the sight of you ker-splonked on the Tarmac with your propeller buried six feet under.

JOHNSON, on his sacking, December 2004

Can't remember what my line on drugs is. What's my line on drugs?

JOHNSON, general election campaign, April 2005

Voting Tory will cause your wife to have bigger breasts and increase your chances of owning a BMW M3.

JOHNSON, general election campaign, April 2005

I'm very attracted to it. I may be diverting from Tory party policy here, but I don't care.

JOHNSON, asked about proposals for 24-hour drinking legislation, general election campaign, April 2005

Oops! Simple Blunders

Life isn't like coursework, baby. It's one damn essay crisis after another.

JOHNSON, writing in the *Daily Telegraph*, May 2005. In December, he was appointed shadow education minister by the new Conservative leader, David Cameron

I'm backing David Cameron's campaign out of pure, cynical self-interest.

JOHNSON on the Conservative Party leadership contest, October 2005

Boris Johnson [is] known as the thinking man's idiot.

HUMPHREY LYTTLETON, *I'm Sorry I Haven't a Clue*, BBC Radio

Come, come. They couldn't hit an elephant at this dist —

American Civil War General JOHN SEDGWICK, last words to his cowering troops, Battle of Spotsylvania, 1864

Thomas — Jefferson — still — surv —

The US President's last words, 1826

2

Eh?

Come Again?

Politicians are at best eccentric communicators. By accident (and sometimes by design) their verbal formulations can lead us not so much to cheer or boo, as to scratch our heads in bewilderment. Often we do realize what they are trying to say. Sometimes they do. But sometimes neither side has the least idea. Mixed emotions and mixed signals produce mixed metaphors and crazy logic and many of those quoted below seem to have confused themselves as much as their audience.

We have leadership – there's just no followership.

GEORGE DANIELSON, US Congressman from California, quoted in the *Wall Street Journal*, December 1979

Nothing happened until I pressed the minister on the floor of the House.

DAVID ALTON, Liberal Chief Whip, 1986

I have not 'singled out' Lothian – I have singled out *four* local councils.

MICHAEL ANCRAM, junior Scottish Office minister, on those delaying sales of council houses, 1987

Social justice is the nation's only hope of salvation . . . Liberating the talent of the people is the nation's only hope of salvation.

TONY BLAIR, same speech, minutes apart, Labour Party conference, September 1999

Eh? Come Again

Leeds is the biggest city of its size in Europe.

GREG MULHOLLAND, Liberal Democrat member for the city, 2005

Er . . . perhaps 'decisive'?

PADDY ASHDOWN, Liberal Democrat leader, on election radio phone-in
responding to questioner who asked, 'Which word best sums up your character?'

Whips do twist their arms up the back literally – and sometimes
physically.

Labour MP JOE ASHTON, *Week in Westminster,* BBC Radio, 1986

Jim Prior's his own man. We all are.

SIR HUMPHREY ATKINS, on Prior's decision to resign as Northern Ireland Secretary,
1984

Deep down I'm a very shallow person.

CHARLES HAUGHEY, Irish Prime Minister

Whatever faults I may have as Secretary of State, making decisions
is not one of them.

STEPHEN BYERS, Transport Secretary, September 2001

Bringing the leadership to its knees occasionally is a good way of
keeping it on its toes.

Labour MP TONY BANKS, on the Conservative leadership struggle, 1990

The Maastricht treaty . . . has been dealt, at least temporarily, a
fatal blow.

DES O'MALLEY, Irish Trade and Commerce minister, on the Danish referendum
rejecting the treaty to create the European Union, June 1992. (Having secured an
opt-out, the Danes re-voted in favour the following year)

Eh? Come Again

Anyone who thinks this country is turning the corner is going round the bend.

NORMAN WILLIS, General Secretary of the Trades Union Congress, 1992

I'd like the taxes to go to those parents lucky enough to have children.

Labour MP TONY BANKS, 1989

Water is a burning issue.

IEUAN OWEN, Welsh Nationalist Plaid Cymru election candidate, Gower, 1982

I think everybody wants safer environments, everybody wants safer streets and everybody will fight to achieve that within our government.

GORDON BROWN, on the Government's approach to dealing with the upsurge of knife crime in Britain, BBC TV interview, January 2008

The bear does not change his spots.

LORD BURNHAM, Conservative defence spokesman in the House of Lords, on Russia, April 1999

Tourists go home with the photographs showing them with one foot in the northern hemisphere and one in the southern.

Geographically challenged ROSIE BARNES, SDP MP for Greenwich, on a famous feature of her constituency, maiden speech in House of Commons, 1987

Many people feel that the Labour Party has gone out on a limb and lost its roots.

BARNES, SDP party political broadcast, BBC Radio, 1987

If you open that Pandora's box, you never know what Trojan 'orses will jump out.

ERNEST BEVIN, Foreign Secretary, on the setting up of the Council of Europe, 1949

❖

The people of Northern Ireland should step back and ask themselves have they moved on.

TONY BLAIR, 2003

❖

We've just had the biggest saturation advertising on record to publicize the sale of water.

TONY BLAIR, Labour shadow spokesman, on water privatization, 1989

❖

I wouldn't be seen dead saying it [that the Conservatives would win the next election].

DAVID BLUNKETT, Labour shadow local government spokesman, 1987

❖

When [the IRA] plant such bombs, it proves they can scare people, it proves they can kill people, it proves nothing.

PETER BOTTOMLEY, Northern Ireland minister, 1990

❖

Suicide is a real threat to health in a modern society.

VIRGINIA BOTTOMLEY, Health Secretary, c. 1993

❖

The Militants in Liverpool spend money like water, as if it came from outer space.

Conservative MP DR RHODES BOYSON, 1987

❖

Clearly, the future is still to come.

PETER BROOKE, 1986

If it weren't for these troubles, Ireland would be a very happy place.

LORD BROOKEBOROUGH, Ulster Minister of Commerce with special responsibilities for tourism, 1970

The streets are safe in Philadelphia, it's only the people who make them unsafe.

FRANK RIZZO, Mayor of Philadelphia, 1972–80

No one would go to Hitler's funeral if he was alive today.

Labour MP RON BROWN, 1989

She wasn't an ardent feminist. She was very beautiful.

Labour MP NORMAN BUCHAN, on the death of socialist Jennie Lee, Labour MP from 1929 to 1970, and wife of Nye Bevan, 1988

If you're at a summit, you're trying to climb a mountain.

LORD CARRINGTON, former Foreign Secretary and 'expert' commentator on the demands of international diplomacy, 1986

❖

We have a lot of kids who don't know what work means. They think work is a four-letter word.

Senator HILLARY CLINTON, speaking to the US Chamber of Commerce, May 2006

❖

It is surprising that the present bitter controversy has arisen between the Government and, on the one hand, the Labour Party – and to some extent the centre parties as well – and, on the other, the British Medical Opposition – British Medical Association. That is certainly my most Freudian slip of the tongue so far.

KENNETH CLARKE, Health Secretary, debate on NHS White Paper, 1989

23

All those people who say that there will never be a single European currency are trying to forecast history.

CLARKE, Chancellor of the Exchequer, c.1993

There remain only twenty-five hours in the day, and Neil Kinnock is already working for twenty-three and a half of them.

ROBIN COOK, Labour shadow spokesman, 1988

There's no smoke without mud being flung around.

EDWINA CURRIE, 1989

I believe that people like myself should stand shoulder to shoulder with the homosexual fraternity . . . but you're only likely to get that support if you don't continue to flaunt your homosexuality and thrust it down other people's throats.

Conservative MP GEOFFREY DICKENS, on militancy in the gay movement, 1988

We're sending 23 million leaflets to every household in Britain.

NORMAN FOWLER, Health Secretary, on the Government's AIDS prevention publicity campaign, 1986

There's a whole range of things we're doing with condoms.

FOWLER, on the AIDS prevention campaign, 1987

I think most of the wrinkles have been ironed out.

Conservative MP TERESA GORMAN, on developments with hormone replacement treatment for older women, 1988

We cannot just sit on our hands. We cannot stand terrified, rooted to the spot.

BRYAN GOULD, Labour shadow trade and industry spokesman, 1987

We're not the sort of party that does deals behind smoke-filled doors.

GOULD, election 1992

My general approach is that you mustn't generalize.

Labour MP HARRIET HARMAN, 1989

My mission is humanitarian. Therefore, it in no way represents the British Government.

EDWARD HEATH, former Prime Minister, on his mission to Baghdad to negotiate the release of Western hostages, Gulf crisis, 1990

We were unanimous – in fact, we were all unanimous.

Liverpool MP ERIC HEFFER, after a meeting of the Labour National Executive Committee, 1982

The essence of being a Prime Minister is to have large ears.

MICHAEL HESELTINE, *Today*, BBC Radio 4, 1990

I went up the greasy pole of politics step by step.

HESELTINE, after his Conservative leadership challenge, 1990

The future, where most of us are destined to spend the rest of our lives . . .

SIR GEOFFREY HOWE, Foreign Secretary, *A Week in Politics*, Channel 4, 1986

That speech must have affected every thinking Conservative MP and many others as well.

DAVID HOWELL, on Sir Geoffrey Howe's resignation speech, critical of Margaret Thatcher, which precipitated her downfall, 1990

Eh? Come Again

As a person, as a human, I understand people's concerns, but as a politician . . .

Tom Harris, Railways Minister, reacting to the payment of huge bonuses for railway managers, February 2008

We will reduce and probably eliminate the homeless by 2008

John Prescott, 2002

There's a lot of overcrowded prisons in the south, and we're planning a new one.

Douglas Hurd, Home Secretary, 1988

I've found the future rather difficult to predict before it happens.

Lord (Roy) Jenkins, 1989

How on earth do the birds know it is a sanctuary?

Conservative MP Sir Keith Joseph, visiting a bird sanctuary

I am concerned that the programmes are so short.

Joseph, when Education Secretary, on a visit to the BBC, which had put together for him a collection of five-minute samples of its schools broadcasts, 1986

Paddy Ashdown was dealt a difficult pack of cards – but he kept his eye on the ball all the way through.

Liberal Democrat (and ex-SDP) MP Charles Kennedy, on Ashdown's first year as party leader, 1989

. . . the haemorrhoid that we have experienced in the last year.

Kennedy, on the membership difficulties of the new Social and Liberal Democrats, successor to the Liberal/SDP Alliance. He meant 'haemorrhage'

Eh? Come Again

There are more crimes in Britain now, due to the huge rise in the crime rate.

NEIL KINNOCK, Labour Party leader, BBC Radio, 1985

Young people by definition have their future before them.

KINNOCK, campaign, 1992

Anyone in his position needs to be whiter than white.

Conservative MP DAME JILL KNIGHT, on Nelson Mandela, Radio Ulster, 1990

One doesn't know how many hot potatoes will appear over the horizon.

DAVID MADEL, Conservative MP, on Leyland cars, 1986

Of course we are not patronizing women. We are just going to explain to them in words of one syllable what it is all about.

LADY OLGA MAITLAND, founder of Women for Peace and a Conservative MP

'If' is a very large preposition.

JOHN MAJOR, 1990

Sustainable growth is growth that is sustainable.

MAJOR, c.1990

Politics is a bit like bicycling. If you keep bicycling, you'll get there in the end.

MAJOR, general election campaign, April 1997

I have learnt from experience that no one can absolutely foresee what will happen in the future.

MAJOR, April 1997

A soundbite never buttered a parsnip.

MAJOR, general election campaign, April 1997

Eh? Come Again

We are not wholly an island, except geographically.

MAJOR, on Britain's place in Europe, c.1992

That part of it is behind us now . . . I'm drawing a line under the sand.

MAJOR, seeking to heal party divisions after the ratification of the Maastricht treaty on the future of Europe, 1992

With the retirement of 'Dickie' Bird, something sad will have gone out of English cricket.

MAJOR, BBC2, 1996

Something that I was not aware had happened turned out to have happened.

MAJOR, explaining the arms-to-Iraq scandal, 1996

In the National Health Service, for years there has been a sterile political debate.

DAVID MELLOR, junior health minister, 1989

Exchange on the Iran–Iraq war:
NICK ROSS, interviewer: It does boil down to a barrel of oil at the end of the day.
David Mellor, foreign office minister: Well, I think that's a crude way of putting it.

BBC Radio 4, 1987

You can argue about that until the cows come home.

ELLIOT MORLEY, environment minister, November 2001, during a radio interview about the animals slaughtered during the foot and mouth outbreak in Britain earlier in the year

There was universal support for it, and very little opposition.

LORD MONTGOMERY, Conservative peer, describing reform of the drink licensing laws, 1987

Eh? Come Again

At the end of the day, isn't it time we called it a day?

JOHN MORRIS, Labour shadow Attorney General, on the government's decision to appeal against its defeat in the *Spycatcher* trial in the Australian courts, 1987

It is at times a minefield.

Labour MP STAN ORME, on the delicacy of the negotiations between the NUM and the National Coal Board during the miners' strike, 1984

The United States, which has a similar type of voting system as ourselves, but very different . . .

DR DAVID OWEN, SDP leader, 1986

We are not prepared to stand idly by and be murdered in our beds.

REV IAN PAISLEY, Ulster Democratic Unionist Party leader, c.1982

I believe that all illegal organizations should be outlawed.

PAISLEY, c.1989

The cost of the Eurotunnel project has risen, but it is usual in these projects and the Anglo-French consortium is looking into ways to bridge the gap.

CECIL PARKINSON, Transport Secretary, 1989

I would expect things to go on much as they are until there is some change.

SIR ANTHONY PARSONS, former ambassador, assessing the Iran–Iraq war, 1984

I've always had a great respect and been very candid with her, and I hope the reverse is the case.

Bath's Conservative MP CHRIS PATTEN, on Margaret Thatcher, 1990

Eh? Come Again

The argument about Labour destroying any prospects of recovery may be *déjà vu* here . . . It's certainly not *déjà vu* in the country. It's very much *vu*. It's very much what er . . . It's very much er . . . shows what sort of an education I had.

PATTEN, then Conservative Party Chairman, campaign, 1992

The absolute rejection of it automatically, a sort of Pavlova's dog reaction, was regrettable.

Liberal MP DAVID PENHALIGON, on the Anglo-Irish peace initiative, 1985

Mothers should encourage their daughters as much as their sons to take up physics and maths. And if they find them difficult, she should say, 'Well, Daddy will help you.'

LADY PLATT, Chairman, Equal Opportunities Commission, *Woman's Hour*, BBC Radio, 1983

When Mrs Thatcher said, 'We are a grandmother,' she was including Denis in her remarks.

LORD PRIOR, former Conservative Cabinet minister, 1989

Trees have to be cut down and replanted.

NICHOLAS RIDLEY, Environment Secretary, 1989

The future is not what it used to be.

MALCOLM RIFKIND, Scottish Secretary, *Talking Politics*, BBC Radio, 1988

Our nuclear power stations are as safe as they can possibly be, and are getting safer all the time.

Environment Minister SIR HUGH ROSSI, 1986

❖

In the wrong hands, samurai swords are dangerous weapons.

Home Office Minister VERNON COAKER, December 2007, on the decision to ban the swords after a rash of attacks using the weapon

But I mustn't go on singling out names. One must not be a name-dropper, as Her Majesty remarked to me yesterday . . .

Conservative MP NORMAN ST JOHN STEVAS, speech to the Museum of the Year Award lunch, reported *Daily Telegraph*, 1979

Remember Nye Bevan: 'I will not go naked into the negotiating table.'

BARONESS SEEAR, Liberal Democrat leader, House of Lords, mis-recalling Bevan's 1957 warning against unilateral nuclear disarmament, 'You will send a Foreign Secretary naked into the conference chamber.' *Question Time*, BBC TV, 1987

The police force in Britain is a reactionary force. It has to respond . . .

Conservative MP MICHAEL SHERSBY, 1990

Headmasters of schools tend to be men.

Labour MP CLARE SHORT, to the party conference, 1990

I had sixteen of them for lunch at the House of Commons.

Rochdale's famously huge Liberal MP CYRIL SMITH, discussing immigrants, 1985

Twice a year, Somerset residents fill Wembley stadium with their rubbish.

CHRIS CLARKE, Leader of Somerset County Council, 1998

Clearly the Prime Minister's devious hand is afoot.

JOHN SMITH, Labour treasury and economic affairs spokesman, 1989

31

Eh? Come Again

To listen to some people in politics, you'd think 'nice' was a four-letter word.

DAVID STEEL, SDP/Liberal Alliance leader, 1986

I think the words 'never' or 'ever' should be avoided by politicians, because you can never foresee what's going to happen.

STEEL, 1987

The fact that we can be in two places at once is a good advantage.

STEEL, on his and David Owen's Liberal Democrat/SDP Alliance election campaign, 1987

You can't manufacture children overnight.

JACK STRAW, Labour education spokesman, *Panorama*, BBC TV, 1990

There is a big difference between 'we will accept these proposals' and 'these proposals are acceptable'.

LABOUR SPOKESMAN, trying to play down the party's enthusiasm for a televised debate between party leaders after strategists decided John Major had more to gain, general election campaign, March 1997

Will this thing jerk me off?

MARGARET THATCHER, firing a field gun during her visit to the Falklands, January 1983

Every Prime Minister needs a Willie.

THATCHER, of William Whitelaw

I am always on the job.

THATCHER, interview on *Aspel and Co*, 1984

Eh? Come Again

Is my right honourable friend saying that Wrens' skirts must be held up until all sailors have been satisfied?

DAME IRENE WARD, responding to the Navy Minister's statement that new uniforms for women would be dealt with as soon as male officers had theirs, House of Commons, 1940

I can have no objections to instruments which merely vibrate.

Speaker BETTY BOOTHROYD, speaking in Commons on pagers, 12 March 1997

I have always said it is a great mistake ever to pre-judge the past.

WILLIAM WHITELAW, on the Ulster political situation, first press conference on becoming Northern Ireland Secretary, 1972

They are going about the country stirring up complacency.

WHITELAW, on Labour ministers, general election campaign, October 1974

I have the thermometer in my mouth and I am listening to it all the time.

WHITELAW, telling reporters how he was monitoring party morale, election campaign, October 1974

I don't blame anyone, except perhaps, all of us.

WHITELAW, Home Secretary, 1980

We are examining alternative anomalies.

WHITELAW, Home Secretary, responding to a proposal that, in view of various anomalies with the TV licence system, he should consider alternatives, 1981

Those who say that I am not in agreement with the policy are, rightly or wrongly, quite wrong.

WHITELAW, on claims that he was not committed to the party's immigration policy

I can assure you that I definitely might take action.

WHITELAW, Home Secretary, giving evidence to a Commons select committee, 1981

Eh? Come Again

I can tell you *exactly* how many trade union members voted for the SDP – about 20 per cent.

SHIRLEY WILLIAMS, founder member of the SDP, election post-mortem, 1983

Certain elements of the British Medical Association leadership have gone over the top and taken fully entrenched positions.

Conservative MP, NICHOLAS WINTERTON, on health reforms, 1989

The idea of a pilot scheme is to see whether it will fly.

LORD YOUNG, Employment Secretary, 1985

Oh look – with hindsight, you can always look back.

LORD YOUNG, deputy Chairman of the Conservative Party and former Trade and Industry Secretary, replying to criticism of the government's handling of the 1985 Harrods/House of Fraser takeover, 1990

The increase in male unemployment for men between 1966 and 1972 can be fully explained by the almost continuous fall in male employment in this period . . .

DEPARTMENT OF EMPLOYMENT's *Employment Gazette*, October 1976

Hazards are one of the main causes of accidents.

US OCCUPATIONAL SAFETY AND HEALTH ADMINISTRATION booklet, 1976

Pesticides in water are derived almost entirely from agricultural and non-agricultural uses.

DRINKING WATER INSPECTORATE for England and Wales, report, April 2001

One important new area is proposed legislation to promote unfair discrimination against people with disabilities.

Forward Look of Government-funded Science, Engineering and Technology, CABINET OFFICE, 1995

We don't want to see these coal fields trampled into the ground.

RODNEY BICKERSTAPFE, general secretary of the National Union of Public Employees (NUPE), during miners' strike, 1984–5

Money is not everything, but it does make poverty tolerable.

MOSS EVANS, general secretary of the Transport and General Workers' Union, after his union contributed to the NUM welfare fund, miners' strike, 1984–5

It'll permanently damage relations for a long time.

JIMMY KNAPP, railwaymen's union leader, on rail dispute, 1985

They blew the talks out of the water before they even got off the ground.

KNAPP, on the British Rail Board, 1989

We haven't demanded anything. What we have demanded is that the coal board withdraw their demands.

ARTHUR SCARGILL, miners' leader, during strike 1984–5

. . . in Poland, or some other South American country.

SCARGILL, *Weekend World*, ITV, interview during miners' strike, 1984–5

The time for balloting is over. It is time to stand up and be counted.

JACK TAYLOR, president of the Yorkshire council of the National Union of Mineworkers, 1983

This is anarchy gone mad.

UNIDENTIFIED UNION OFFICIAL complaining that action by another union had been taken without consultation, during the Winter of Discontent, 1979

[The green belt] It's a Labour achievement and we intend to build on it.

JOHN PRESCOTT, Deputy Prime Minister, quoted in the *Guardian*, April 1999

Meditation.

JOHN PRESCOTT, Labour's Deputy Leader, suggesting a solution to a fire service dispute in Essex, general election campaign, April 1997. He intended to say mediation

I have probably known Michael Heseltine longer than anyone else for the last 16 years.

CHAIRMAN OF THE HENLEY-ON-THAMES CONSERVATIVE ASSOCIATION, during the party leadership election, 1990

The report speaks for itself. It's a very good report. It's a very long report. I haven't read the report.

KEITH VAZ, Labour MP, BBC radio interview on the report of the committee of enquiry into the outbreak in Britain of foot and mouth disease, 2001

I may not know about industry or about agriculture, but when it comes to water I can certainly hold my own.

UNIDENTIFIED DELEGATE, debate on water authorities, following debates on industry and agriculture, Conservative Party conference, 1980

I'm sorry I missed the first course. I've been doing drugs most of the day.

MO MOWLAM, minister in charge of the government's drugs policy, arriving late at a charity lunch, November 2000

Eh? Come Again

There is no housing shortage in Lincoln today – just a rumour that is put about by people who have nowhere to live.

COUNCILLOR MURFIN, Lord Mayor of Lincoln

I would not say most of them, but certainly the majority.

UNIDENTIFIED GWYNEDD COUNTY COUNCILLOR, estimating the number of Welsh-speaking police officers, 1987

Islam is not a pacifist religion. Islam will hit back, and sometimes hit back first.

KALIM SADDIQUI, spokesman for militant Muslim organization, on the Salman Rushdie *Satanic Verses* controversy, 1989

Conservative policies are the country's most important discovery since the advent of circumcised nans.

Conservative Party slogan ('The best invention since sliced bread') translated into Punjabi for the 1983 general election. It was spotted by a last-minute proof check, and never circulated

Can it possibly be an act of aggression to anticipate something that would be lawful in twelve years' time?

Labour MP TONY BENN, legally quixotic view on Nasser's seizure of the Suez canal, 1956. (The Anglo-French concession on the canal was due to revert to Egypt in 1968)

There's so much more to nick.

DOUGLAS HURD, Home Secretary, giving his explanation for the rise in crime, 1987

We need more inequality in order to eliminate poverty.

SIR KEITH JOSEPH, 1975

37

Eh? Come Again

In 1948, a Washington radio station contacted ambassadors in the capital, asking what each would most like for Christmas. Britain's representative, Sir Oliver Franks, mistook the request.

French Ambassador: Peace throughout the world.

Soviet Ambassador: Freedom for all people enslaved by imperialism.

Sir Oliver: Well, it's very kind of you to ask. I'd quite like a box of crystallized fruit.

I am not quite certain what my right honourable friend said, but we both hold precisely the same view.

Prime Minister MARGARET THATCHER, Question Time, House of Commons, January 1989

RONALD MILLER (speechwriter to MRS THATCHER, giving her encouragement moments before her first speech to the Party conference as leader, 1975): 'Piece of cake, Margaret.'

Thatcher: Good heavens! Not *now*.

Keep taking the pills.

MARGARET THATCHER's intended re-draft of a joke in her speech to the party conference in 1977. Prime Minister Jim Callaghan had lately been reported as seeing himself as Moses leading the country out of the wilderness. Thatcher's speechwriters had included the line, 'So my message to Moses is, Keep taking the tablets.' The speechwriting team realized that she had never understood the joke. They persuaded her to keep to the original

We have become a grandmother.

THATCHER, announcing the birth of her grandson, 1989

We said zero, and I think any statistician will tell you that when you're dealing with very big numbers, zero must mean plus or minus a few.

WILLIAM WALDEGRAVE, Health Secretary, on hospital waiting lists, election campaign, 1992

Eh? Come Again

Rates: this was once a problem for the rich. Because Socialism has improved our way of life, it is now a problem for everybody.

LABOUR MANIFESTO, district council elections, Forest of Dean, 1976

The real lesson of this . . . is that women of all social classes are vulnerable to attack by men.

Labour Herald, after intruder Michael Fagan had managed to enter Buckingham Palace and get into the Queen's bedroom, July 1982

The Alliance will reduce employment by one million in three years.

SDP/LIBERAL ALLIANCE ELECTION LEAFLET, Chesterfield, 1987: 38,000 were distributed before what the party's agent described as the 'typing error' was noticed

Angela Rumbold believes in preventing unnecessary crime.

CONSERVATIVE LEAFLET, Mitcham and Morden, 1997 general election campaign

If members cannot get into work tomorrow because of the weather, we may have to postpone the walk-out.

CIVIL SERVICE UNION OFFICIAL, Navy Department, Bath, during the 'Winter of Discontent', 1979

Sir Geoffrey drove to within a stone's throw of Mrs Mandela's house.

BBC RADIO 4 NEWS, on Foreign Secretary Geoffrey Howe's visit to South Africa during the height of civil disturbances, 1986

I'm joined now by Trevor McDonald who is down at the summit.

PETER SISSONS, newsreader, Channel 4 news, 1986

The Alliance always does better when people actually vote for it.

PETER HOBDAY, presenter, *Today,* BBC Radio (discussing tactical voting), 1986

Eh? Come Again

It will be the first time the two countries [England and Argentina] have met in a major sporting event since the Falklands War in 1982.

BBC RADIO 4 news, previewing the soccer World Cup quarter-final, 1986

This is the worst disaster in California since I was elected.

PAT BROWN, state Governor 1959–1967, on a local flood crisis

The Prime Minister was said to be very concerned about the large amount of litter as she swept down the M4 recently.

BBC RADIO 4, 1986

Mr Kinnock's talks with President Reagan could hardly be described as a meeting of minds.

Today news report, BBC Radio 4, 1987

Experts will be on hand in the studio to make sense of what the Chancellor said.

DAVID DIMBLEBY, previewing Budget Special, BBC TV, 1988

The Minister Lord Caithness, responsible for the policy of openness, refused to talk about it on this programme.

Face the Facts, BBC Radio 4, 1988

Paul Channon is sacked and Tony Newton gets social security.

ITV NEWSFLASH announcing Cabinet reshuffle, 1989

Sir Thomas More, as well as a politician, was also a thinker.

MARGARET HOWARD, BBC Radio 4, 1990

Eh? Come Again

10,500 more policemen are helping the police with their enquiries.

Misfiring CONSERVATIVE ELECTION POSTER, 1987, intended to highlight the government's record for increasing police numbers. One party supporter commented that 'They seem to be trying to tell us there are more bent coppers than before.' The party's advertising agency said that it was 'not sure this one has worked'

One reason I changed the Labour Party is so that we can remain true to our principles.

TONY BLAIR, general election campaign, April 1997

What this country needs is good farmers, good businessmen and good plumbers.

RICHARD NIXON's farewell speech, 1974

I know you believe you understand what you think I said, but I'm not sure you realize that what you've heard is not what I meant.

NIXON

I'm a great fan of baseball. I watch a lot of games on the radio.

President GERALD FORD

There is no Soviet domination of Eastern Europe, and there never will be under a Ford Administration.

GERALD FORD, incumbent President, TV debate, campaign 1976

I don't believe that the Poles consider themselves dominated by the Soviet Union . . . Each of those countries [of Eastern Europe] is independent, autonomous, it has its own territorial integrity and the United States does not concede that those countries are under the domination of the Soviet Union.

FORD, elaborating his previous answer, 1976

Eh? Come Again

We are going to make certain to the best of our ability that any allegation of domination is not a fact.

FORD, attempting to clarify his stance, 1976

I did not express myself clearly – I admit.

FORD, explaining himself to a delegation of Eastern European ethnic organizations, 1976

I hope my relationship with them will grow after this embryonic start.

Democratic candidate, JIMMY CARTER, after outlining his views on abortion to Roman Catholic bishops, campaign, 1976

. . . a great man who should have been President and would have been one of the greatest Presidents in history – Hubert Horatio Hornblower . . . er Humphrey.

President JIMMY CARTER, paying tribute to the recently deceased party elder statesman, Democratic convention, 1980

The United States has much to offer the Third World War.

RONALD REAGAN, presidential candidate, speaking on the third world, 1975. He used the phrase no fewer than nine times in the speech

Our security and our hopes for success at the arms reduction talks hinge on the determination that we show to continue our programme to rebuild and refortify our defences.

REAGAN, President, 1985

Facts are stupid things.

REAGAN, outgoing President, addressing the Republican national convention, 1988. He was quoting a previous President, John Adams, 'Facts are stubborn things.' He repeated the mistake several times

Now we are trying to get unemployment to go up, and I think we are going to succeed.

REAGAN, 1982

Eh? Come Again

We spend weeks and hours every day preparing the budget.
REAGAN, 1987

There's something about . . . having a horse between my knees that makes it easier to sort out a problem.
REAGAN, autobiography, *An American Life,* 1990

Trees cause more pollution than cars.
REAGAN, 1981

You can believe me. I'm not smart enough to lie.
REAGAN, on the US presidential election stump, 1980

It's no exaggeration to say the undecideds could go one way or the other.
GEORGE BUSH SNR, during presidential campaign, 1988

I believe in unions and I believe in non-unions.
BUSH SNR, campaign 1988

I don't know what he means, but I disagree with him.
BUSH SNR, responding to a journalist's question during the Gulf crisis, 1990

I have opinions of my own – strong opinions – but I don't always agree with them.
BUSH SNR

We have had triumphs, we have made mistakes, we have had sex.
BUSH SNR, on his eight years as Ronald Reagan's Vice-President, Republican national convention, 1988. He meant to say, 'we have had setbacks'

I stand for anti-bigotry, anti-semitism and anti-racism.
BUSH SNR, campaign, 1988

Eh? Come Again

When I was growing up, with was a dangerous world, we knew exactly who the they were. It was us versus them, and it was clear who the them was were. Today, we are not so sure who the they are, but we know they're there.

Presidential candidate GEORGE W. BUSH, campaign speech to Iowa Western Community College, January 2000, one of the earliest realisations by the world's press of Bush's now legendary struggle with the English language

I want it to be said that the Bush administration was a results-oriented administration, because I believe the results of focusing our attention and energy on teaching children to read and having an education system that's responsive to the child and to the parents . . . will make America what we want it to be, a literature country and a hopefuller country.

BUSH, shortly before his second inauguration, January 2001

You teach a child to read and he or her will be able to pass a literacy test.

BUSH, speaking at a junior school in Tennessee, February 2001

I'm honored to be here with the eternal general of the United States, mi amigo Alberto Gonzales.

BUSH, introducing the Attorney General at a White House ceremony, May 2007

Make no mistake about it, I understand how tough it is, sir. I talk to families who die.

BUSH, December 2006

Our enemies are innovative and resourceful, and so are we. They never stop thinking about new ways to harm our country and our people, and neither do we.

BUSH, Washington press conference, August 2004

I promise you I will listen to what has been said here, even though I wasn't here.

BUSH, at the President's Economic Forum, Texas, August 2002

Eh? Come Again

The solution to Iraq [is] an Iraq that can govern itself, sustain itself and defend itself . . . Precisely the reason why I sent more troops into Baghdad.
<small>BUSH, April 2007</small>

Iraqis are sick of foreign people coming in their country and trying to destabilize their country, and we will help them rid Iraq of these killers.
<small>BUSH, on the Iraqi insurgency, 2004, all irony lost</small>

This notion that the United States is getting ready to attack Iran is simply ridiculous. And having said that, all options are on the table.
<small>BUSH, NATO meeting, Brussels, February 2005</small>

We do know of certain knowledge that he is either in Afghanistan or in some other country or dead. And we know of certain knowledge that we don't know, which of those happens to be the case.
<small>DONALD RUMSFELD, US Defense Secretary, press conference, December 2001</small>

We expect [the Salvadorans] to work toward the elimination of human rights.
<small>DAN QUAYLE, Vice-President</small>

We're going to have the best-educated American people in the world.
<small>QUAYLE</small>

One word sums up probably the responsibility of any Vice-President. And that one word is, 'to be prepared'
<small>QUAYLE</small>

[Republicans] understand the importance of bondage between parent and child.
<small>QUAYLE, campaign, 1988. He meant 'bonding'</small>

Eh? Come Again

The Nazi holocaust was an obscene period in our country's history . . . well, not our country's history, this century's history . . . we all lived in this century; I didn't live in this century . . .

QUAYLE, campaign, 1988

There's a lot of uncharted waters in space.

QUAYLE, c.1989

The only regret I have was that I didn't study Latin harder in school so I could converse with those people.

QUAYLE, on visit to Latin America, 1989 (attrib.)

May our nation continue to be a beakon [sic] of hope to the world . . .

Greeting inscribed on 30,000 of QUAYLE's Christmas cards sent, 1989

There is an irreversible trend to freedom and democracy in Eastern Europe. But this may change.

QUAYLE, speech to the Newspaper Society forum on Europe, 1990

If we do not succeed, then we run the risk of failure.

QUAYLE, speech to Arizona Republicans, 1990

Hawaii is a unique state. It is a small state. It is a state that is by itself. It is a . . . it is different than the other forty-nine states. Well, all states are different, but it's got a particularly unique situation.

QUAYLE, campaigning in Hawaii, 1992

Mars is essentially in the same orbit. Mars is somewhat the same distance from the sun, which is very important. We have seen pictures where there are canals, we believe, and water. If there is water, that means there is oxygen. If oxygen, that means we can breathe.

QUAYLE

It's better than some of the grades I got in school.

QUAYLE, responding to former Vice-President Walter Mondale's rating of his performance as 'tepid C', August 1989

46

Eh? Come Again

What a waste it is to lose one's mind – or not to have a mind.
QUAYLE, 1989

Unfortunately, the people of Louisiana are not racists.
QUAYLE

Another dark horse candidate, President James Knox.
Response by vice-presidential candidate AL GORE when asked to name a past US President from whom he drew personal inspiration, campaign, 1992. (There has not been a President Knox.)

Life is very important to Americans.
Senate leader BOB DOLE, on being asked whether American lives were more important than foreign lives

I strongly support the feeding of children.
President GERALD FORD, endorsing a School Lunch Bill

Many Americans don't like the simple things. That's what they have against we conservatives.
BARRY GOLDWATER, Republican candidate, campaigning in the presidential election, 1964. Goldwater's repeated verbal gaffes led to his press aide pleading with the press corps, 'Don't quote what he says – quote what he means'

No, thank you. I'd much rather watch you in bed with my wife.
GOLDWATER, declining the offer from a famous American chat show host to become a regular on the programme

Wherever I have gone in this country, I have found Americans.
ALFRED LANDON, Republican challenger to Roosevelt, campaign, 1936

Americans have the best system in the world: they've just got to find a way to make it work.

Vice-President NELSON ROCKEFELLER, 1975

The chief problem of the low-income farmers is poverty.

ROCKEFELLER, Governor of New York, 1960

Get this thing straight once and for all. The policeman is not there to *create* disorder. The policeman is there to *preserve* disorder.

RICHARD DALEY, Mayor of Chicago, attempting to refute brutality allegations against his police during the riotous 1968 Democratic convention

We shall reach greater and greater platitudes of achievement.

DALEY

When more and more people are thrown out of work, unemployment results.

CALVIN COOLIDGE, former US President, 1930

The only way the Republican Party can hold the White House ... is to nominate a candidate who can win.

ALEXANDER HAIG, former US Secretary of State, campaign 1988

Drinking is a major cause of psoriasis.

DONNA SHALALA, US Health and Human Services Secretary, mistaking the skin disease for the liver disease cirrhosis, April 1993

A nuclear power plant is infinitely safer than eating, because 300 people choke to death on food every year.

DIXIE LEE RAY, Governor of Washington State, 1977

Eh? Come Again

You people are exemplifying what my brother meant when he said in his inaugural address, 'Ask what you can do for – uh – do not ask what you can do – uh – ask not what you can do for your country but –' Well, anyhow, you remember his words.

ROBERT KENNEDY, US Attorney-General, to the Foreign Student Service Council, 1962. He concluded his embarrassment: 'That's why my brother is President'

The police are fully able to meet and compete with the criminals.

JOHN HYLAN, Mayor of New York, during a crime wave, 1922

We are going to have peace even if we have to fight for it.

President DWIGHT D. EISENHOWER

It's the most unheard-of thing I've ever heard of.

Senator JOSEPH MCCARTHY, asked to comment on an allegation made in one of his un-American Activities Committee hearings during the early 1950s

This is a delightful surprise to the extent that it is a surprise and it is only a surprise to the extent that we anticipated.

JAMES BAKER, US Secretary of State, on the Kohl-Gorbachev agreement on German reunification, July 1990

Your food stamps will be stopped effective March 1992 because we received notice that you passed away. May God bless you. You may reapply if there is a change in your circumstances.

Letter sent by Greenville County Department of Social Services, South Carolina, to resident two weeks after his death, March 1992

I want to thank each and every one of you for having extinguished yourselves this session.

GIB LEWIS, speaker of the Texas House of Representatives

Eh? Come Again

This will mean a sea change in Atlantic relationships.

HENRY KISSINGER, 1986

The United States looks upon Mexico as a good neighbour, a strong upholder of democratic traditions in this hemisphere and a country we are proud to call our own.

EDWARD STETTINIUS, US Secretary of State, arriving in Mexico City for an official visit, February 1945. Officials quickly issued a correction, changing 'own' to 'friend'

This strategy represents our policy for all time. Until it's changed.

MARLIN FITZWATER, White House press spokesman, on the Bush administration's national security policy, 1990

The only way we'll ever get a volunteer army is to draft them.

F. EDWARD HERBERT, Chairman of the House Committee on Armed Services

Conservatives must win the next election – not for ourselves, but for the hard-working, law-abiding people of Britain.

IAIN DUNCAN-SMITH, short-lived Conservative party leader 2001–2003

Capital punishment is our society's recognition of the sanctity of human life.

ORRIN G. HATCH, US Senator for Utah, 1988

You just can't let nature run wild.

WALTER HICKEL. Governor of Alaska, 1966–69, explaining his order to state officials to cull hundreds of wolves in the wilderness

I don't want to run the risk of ruining what is a lovely recession.

GEORGE BUSH SNR, responding to a welcoming crowd, New Jersey, campaign, 1992. He meant 'reception'

Eh? Come Again

Now let's all try to settle this problem like good Christians.

WARREN AUSTIN, US delegate to the United Nations, on the Arab-Israeli war, 1948

Those who survived the San Francisco earthquake said, 'Thank God, I'm still alive.' But of course, those who died, their lives will never be the same again.

BARBARA BOXER, Californian member of US House of Representatives, 1989

... the need to establish a democratic, legal, circular state.

Press announcement issued by the AZERBAIJAN EMBASSY in London, followed the next day by another explaining, 'The word circular should be read as secular', 1995

We must organize now.

ALEXANDER SHUBIN, leader of Russian anarchists, June 1990

It is difficult to make predictions, particularly about the future.

Representative of the United Nations High Commissioner for Refugees, 1990

Sixty years of progress, without change.

Slogan used by Saudi Arabian government to promote the kingdom's sixtieth anniversary, October 1992

Let Us Trim Our Hair in Accordance with Socialist Lifestyle.

Title of a TV series in NORTH KOREA, where the government was directing men to see their barbers twice a month, January 2005.

I cannot say, and do not know whether the coming quota will be the same, more, or less than the previous one. But the tonnage will definitely fall within one of these three options.

Yosmo OKAWARA, Japanese ambassador to Australia, on the beef quota, 1977

Eh? Come Again

All I was doing was appealing for an endorsement, not suggesting you endorse it.

GEORGE BUSH SNR, to Colorado governor, campaign, 1992

We will not be abolishing the right to buy schooling: it is just that they [parents] will have to buy it abroad.

Party Leader NEIL KINNOCK, on Labour's policy to abolish fee-paying schools, general election, 1983

The growth of post neo-classical endogenous growth theory and the symbiotic relationships between growth and investment.

GORDON BROWN, Labour Shadow Chancellor, 1994

We want to deliver an action plan which is evidence-based, action-oriented, takes an end-to-end approach and provides a basis for positive action.

PAUL GOGGINS, junior Home Office minister, announcing in the House of Commons the government's strategy against people-smuggling, July 2005

We are not legislating now on the basis that we are bringing it in now for something that might happen in the future. We are putting in a provision for it if it becomes unhypothetical.

Home Secretary JACQUI SMITH attempting to explain the reasoning behind proposals to extend detention periods for terrorist suspects, January 2008

❖

A multi-agency project catering for holistic diversionary provision to young people for positive action.

LUTON EDUCATION AUTHORITY's description of go-karting lessons, November 2000

❖

Democracy is more important than having a parliament.

DR PETER ONU, acting Secretary-General of the Organization of African Unity, 1985

Eh? Come Again

With these few words I want to assure you that I love you and if you had been a woman I would have considered marrying you, although your head is full of grey hairs, but as you are a man that possibility doesn't arise.

Ugandan President IDI AMIN in a letter to Tanzanian President Julius Nyerere, 1972

That canard was introduced as a red herring.

Former Jamaican Prime Minister MICHAEL MANLEY, 1983

Our Cabinet is always unanimous — except when we disagree.

WILLIAM VANDER ZALM, Premier of British Columbia, Canada

We are doing everything we would normally be doing, but more of it.

ISRAELI MILITARY SPOKESMAN seeking to play down the army's state of alert, Jerusalem, October 1990

The Kurds who are being executed do not belong to the Kurdish people.

AYATOLLAH KHOMEINI, Iranian spiritual leader

I intend to open the country up to democracy, and anyone who is against that I will jail, I will crush.

PRESIDENT JOÃO FIGUEIREDO of Brazil, on his inauguration, 1979

Carter apparently doesn't even know that Michigan is one of the forty-eight states.

GERALD FORD, campaigning for Ronald Reagan, 1980. Told there were fifty, he recovered: 'I voted for Hawaii and Alaska [to become states] and I'm proud of it.'

Eh? Come Again

When Japan tells us 'yes', often it means 'no'. It is very important for the Japanese not to behave the same to you.

Boris Yeltsin advising Bill Clinton during US–Russian summit, Vancouver, April 1993. The White House later clarified the remarks as being 'casual comments about Japanese courtesy and etiquette'

No.

Tohei Kono, Japanese government spokesman, asked whether Japanese often mean 'no' when they say 'yes', April 1993

The information was correct, but the interpretations were not. I did my duty up to the last minute.

Mohammed Saeed al-Sahhaf, former Iraqi Information Minister (aka Comical Ali), who spoke of an Iraqi victory even as US troops were approaching Baghdad, speaking on Arab television, July 2003

Following a nuclear attack on the United States, the United States Postal Service plans to distribute Emergency Change of Address Cards.

Executive Order 11490, US Federal Emergency Management Agency, October 1969

Every effort will be made to clear . . . [cheques], including those drawn on destroyed banks. You will be encouraged to buy US Savings Bonds.

Executive Order 11490, on plans to handle a nuclear attack, US Federal Emergency Management Agency,1969

The destruction of Clapham Junction will entail London Transport providing a shuttle bus service between the London centre and the undamaged part of the railway line south of Clapham. It is estimated that 500 buses could be withdrawn for the removal of the homeless. This could cause severe delay in getting workers home . . . .

From a 1952 study of the effects of a nuclear strike on London, released by the Public Record Office in 2001

It is assumed that all [evacuation] centres will hold sufficient stock for the first tea-making.

From the same document

It contains a misleading impression, not a lie. It was being economical with the truth.

SIR ROBERT ARMSTRONG, Cabinet Secretary and head of the Civil Service, giving evidence in the *Spycatcher* trial, Sydney, November 1986

I have lied in good faith.

BERNARD TAPIE, former French minister, on trial for corruption, March 1995

Just because Europe adopts the euro is no reason why we should! We have a much older history!

MARGARET THATCHER, election campaign, May 2001

We are, in a way, for Iraq and against Kuwait, and also for Kuwait and against Iraq.

FAISAL HUSSEINI, PLO spokesman, on Palestinian Gulf War loyalties, August 1990

I want blacks to feel that they are part of this country's existence. They are as much welcome at Buckingham Palace as anywhere else.

PRINCE CHARLES, 1982

We are sitting on a powder keg which could explode in our faces at any time.

DESMOND TUTU, Archbishop of Cape Town, on the political situation in South Africa, 1985

It is a transparent smokescreen.

South African Conservative Party judgement on the government's plans for political reform, 1990

Sometimes you can have competing election promises.

MALCOLM FRASER, future Australian Prime Minister, general election, 1976

We can beat the Liberals even with one engine tied behind our back.

JOE CLARK, Conservative Prime Minister of Canada, 1979–80

Why did they have to build the damn lake so close to the city?

MICHAEL KENNA, early 20th century Chicago politician, on Lake Michigan (attrib.)

If this letter contains your correct address you do not need to do anything. If the address on this letter is wrong, please tell us your correct details.

Instructions sent out by the PENSIONS SERVICE, 2002

A government is not an old pair of socks that you throw out. Come to think of it, you don't throw out old pairs of socks anyway these days.

BORIS YELTSIN, Russian President, dismissing calls for his resignation, January 1992

The Israeli intelligence community is more open today than it has ever been. This is stated by a top military intelligence officer, Colonel 'A', who was speaking to our correspondent.

Israeli Defence Forces Radio, 1984

3

Shh!

Giving the Game Away

'Far better,' Norman Tebbit once snapped at an opponent, 'keep your mouth shut and let everyone think you're stupid, than open it and remove all doubt.' Cats out of bags – what the press call 'gaffes' – are often no more than flashes of lucidity, honesty or dangerous ambiguity. These can be fatal in public life. However tactless, those quoted below usually believed what they said. In some cases, they were horribly wrong, in others horribly right. A few would still stand by their remarks – and some may even be admired for their courage. But in most cases, it may be doubted (though not necessarily by them) whether they were wise to share their thoughts . . .

A Conservative government is an organized hypocrisy.

BENJAMIN DISRAELI, future Conservative Prime Minister, opposing his own government on the Corn Laws, 1845

I never knew the lower classes had such white skins.

Alleged remark by LORD CURZON, member of the War Cabinet and former Viceroy of India, touring the Western Front during the First World War and seeing soldiers bathing

He is used to dealing with estate workers. I cannot see how anyone can say he is out of touch.

LADY CAROLINE DOUGLAS-HOME, Sir Alec's daughter, defending her father's credentials for the prime ministership, 1963

Shh! Giving the Game Away

I would never do anything to deride the profession of politics – although I think it is a form of madness.

LORD HOME, former Prime Minister, 1983

Terrible intrusion in one's private life.

LORD HOME, reflecting on being Prime Minister, 1989

I was Chancellor of the Exchequer . . . for five years and . . . I never understood it.

WINSTON CHURCHILL, 1951, on appointing John Boyd-Carpenter to a junior Ministerial post at the Treasury

There are only two types of chancellor: those who fail and those who get out just in time.

GORDON BROWN, Chancellor from 1997 who got out to become Prime Minister in June 2007

I know a great deal more about the world today than I ever did in government.

JOHN MAJOR, former Prime Minister, April 2007, ten years after leaving office

When I'm sitting on the woolsack in the House of Lords, I amuse myself by saying 'bollocks' sotto voce to the bishops.

LORD HAILSHAM, Lord Chancellor, 1985

❖

We have screwed up. Not a little but a lot. No country in Europe has screwed up as much as we have. It can be explained. We have obviously lied throughout the past 18 to 24 months. It was perfectly clear that what we were saying was not true . . . I almost perished because I had to pretend for 18 months that we were governing. Instead, we lied morning, noon and night.

FERENC GYURCSANY, Hungarian Prime Minister, speech to a private meeting of his party a few weeks after being returned to office in a general election in April 2006. A tape of the comments was broadcast in September leading to riots in Budapest. He survived the scandal

Shh! Giving the Game Away

I asked Boris Yeltsin to tell me briefly what the situation in Russia was like. 'Good,' he said. I asked for a longer version. 'Not good,' he replied.

JOHN MAJOR, former Prime Minister, reminiscing, November 1999

It is true that liberty is precious – so precious that it must be rationed.

LENIN (attrib. by Sidney and Beatrice Webb, 1936)

A single death is a tragedy, a million deaths is a statistic.

JOSEPH STALIN (attrib.)

We are not without accomplishment. We have managed to distribute poverty equally.

NGUYEN CO THACH, Foreign Minister, Communist Vietnam

All they want is a tight c**t, loose shoes and a warm place to shit.

EARL BUTZ, US Agriculture Secretary, campaigning for President Ford, questioned why his Republican Party had not recruited more blacks, 1976

We have every kind of mixture you can have. I have a black, I have a woman, two Jews and a cripple.

JAMES WATT, US Interior Secretary, on the balanced composition of an advisory group, 1983. The remark cost him his job

As far as the politics of Wales is concerned, as of 48 hours ago I knew absolutely nothing. I now know nothing, plus a bit.

LORD GLENTORAN on his qualifications on being appointed Conservative spokesman on Wales in the House of Lords, July 2007

Shh! Giving the Game Away

The other week I read a story in the *Daily Express* that I was going to sack all junior ministers over 52. Wondered where it came from, and then suddenly remembered I'd leaked it myself.

HAROLD WILSON, quoted by John Junor, editor of the *Express*

If the criminal wants to commit suicide, then he should be allowed to do so. Something should be left in the cell. Perhaps a razor blade.

JONATHAN GUINNESS, (unsuccessful) Conservative candidate, Lincoln by-election, 1973

I wouldn't say she was open-minded on the Middle East so much as empty-headed. For instance, she probably thinks that Sinai is the plural of sinus.

Conservative MP JONATHAN AITKEN, on Margaret Thatcher during the party leadership election, 1975

He didn't riot. He got on his bike and looked for work.

Conservative MP NORMAN TEBBIT, on his father's attitude to unemployment, Conservative Party conference, 1981

We can beat them in the 1980s and 1990s. We have beaten them in other respects and we can do it again.

JOHN BUTCHER, junior Trade and Industry minister, on Japan, 1984

Bongo Bongo land.

ALAN CLARK, Employment Minister, referring to the origins of an African delegation, 1985

❖

Absolute bollocks.

BOB AINSWORTH, Armed Forces Minister, interjecting in the speech of opposition MP Tony Baron who was criticising the Government for shortages of equipment in the army, House of Commons, January 2008. Regretably for posterity, the exchange was 'tidied up' for the official record. It now reads in Hansard merely as 'interruption'

Shh! Giving the Game Away

There is nothing I can do for him professionally.

Ron Brown MP's fellow Labour MP, SAM GALBRAITH, a brain surgeon

I always vote for the Tories. They are my best clients.

NORMA LEVY, prostitute at the centre of the Lord Lambton scandal, 1973

I'm not prejudiced against gays and lesbians but there is no point in trying to delude myself that I feel anything but revulsion at the idea of touching another man.

DAVID BLUNKETT

At least if I'd been f**king somebody I would have been having some fun.

Conservative MP ALAN DUNCAN, commenting on allegations that a property deal had been 'scandalous', 1995

The Cricket Test – which side do they cheer for?

NORMAN TEBBIT, patriarch of the Conservative right, introducing a new yardstick for successful racial integration, 1990

A German racket to take over the whole of Europe. It has to be thwarted.

NICHOLAS RIDLEY, Trade and Industry Secretary, on European monetary union, interview in the *Spectator*, 1990. He resigned within days

Bastards

JOHN MAJOR, caught on-camera and off-guard describing the Euro-sceptics in his party, 1994

Shh! Giving the Game Away

We need to get a handle on this, will you ring those f***ers.

New Irish Prime Minister, BRIAN COWEN, giving instructions to his female Deputy, inadvertently picked up by microphones in the Irish Parliament during Leader's Questions, May 2008, two weeks after becoming Premier. A spokesman asserted that it had been 'a casual exchange between working colleagues'. The abusive comment was said to refer to civil servants, not other members of the House. Cowen, notorious for being a political bruiser, rejoices in the nickname BIFFO - Big Ignorant F***er From Offaly

They are all the same. They're short, they're fat and they are fundamentally corrupt.

ROD RICHARDS, junior Welsh Office minister, on Welsh Labour councillors, 1995

He wants our advice.

Note written by Tory whip DAVID WILLETTS about a supposedly independent Select Committee chairman Sir Geoffrey Johnson Smith. Mr Willetts explained he meant the Chairman was 'in want' of advice. His excuse was not accepted and Mr Willetts was found guilty of 'dissembling'

I wish that cow would resign.

RICHARD NEEDHAM, Northern Ireland Minister, on his car telephone to his wife, airing his views on the Prime Minister, 1990. The call was overheard and recorded by a radio eavesdropper. (He later telephoned Mrs Thatcher and apologized.)

If there is one thing that really pisses me off, it's middle class whingers going on about f**king tuition fees and as far as I'm concerned, if that's your attitude, you can shove your vote up your a**e.

STEPHEN POUND, Labour MP for Ealing North, 2001 General Election, leaving a message on a constituent's answerphone in response to her call enquiring about Labour education policy. He was returned with an increased majority

If any of you have got an A-level, it is because you have worked to get it. Go to any other country and when you have got an A-level, you have bought it.

MICHAEL PORTILLO, Chief Secretary to the Treasury, speech to students at Southampton University, February 1994

There's a lot that can be done in terms of encouraging more people to enjoy a cheap and cheerful service at one moment in the day for the typists and perhaps a more luxurious service for the civil servants and businessmen who might travel at a slightly different time.

ROGER FREEMAN, public transport minister, infuriating secretaries, 1992

You have your own company, your own temperature control, your own music and you don't have to put up with dreadful human beings sitting alongside you.

STEVEN NORRIS, Minister of Transport, favouring the private car over public transport, February 1995

Most [street beggars] are Scottish and I've never met one yet who politely and gently asked for money . . . There are no genuine beggars. Those who are in need have got all the social benefits they require . . . Beggars are doing so out of choice because they find it more pleasant . . . I always give them something – I give them a piece of my mind.

DAVID MACLEAN, then Home Office minister, January 1997. In response to criticism of his remarks, he said: 'As any sensible person would appreciate, I meant no insult to the Scottish people', January 1997

I wouldn't walk around at midnight and I'm fortunate that I don't have to … I just don't think that's a thing that people do, is it really?

JACQUI SMITH, Home Secretary and the minister responsible for Britain's policing, admitting in a press interview that the streets of London were too dangerous to walk alone at night, January 2008

Crikey!

SIR NORMAN FOWLER, Health Secretary, wiping his brow when a civil servant, advising on the spread of AIDS, explained to him what oral sex was (attrib.)

Shh! Giving the Game Away

[You have] to use the resources you've got to make any occupation totally untenable.

NEIL KINNOCK, explaining Labour's defence policy during general election campaign, 1987, widely interpreted as contemplating invasion of Britain and a guerrilla warfare strategy

If we had the death penalty, [they] would have been forgotten [and] we shouldn't have had all these campaigns to get them released.

LORD DENNING, former Master of the Rolls, August 1990, on the case of the Birmingham Six, jailed for life in 1975 for allegedly being responsible for an IRA bombing in the city. They were released in 1991 after the verdicts were declared unsafe by the Appeal Court

I think in a fair tax system, people like me would pay a bit more tax.

CLARE SHORT, April 1996

It would be mischievous to see my remark as a call for higher taxes for people on middle incomes.

SHORT, 'clarifying' statement issued later same day

I will not be silenced.

SHORT, the next day

They lack fragrance on the whole. They're definitely not desert island material . . . They all look as though they are from the 5th Kiev Stalinist machine-gun parade.

Eccentric right-wing Conservative MP SIR NICHOLAS FAIRBAIRN, deprecating the lack of style of women MPs

What's a skirt but an open gateway?

FAIRBAIRN

Shh! Giving the Game Away

The TUC is not involved in party politics. Nor is its General Secretary . . . I hope that every trade unionist with a vote in Walsall, Workington and Newcastle will cast it next Thursday for the Labour candidate.

TUC General Secretary, LEN MURRAY, before three by-elections, 1976

Liberty is conforming to the majority.

HUGH SCANLON, Engineering Workers' Union leader, 1977

Politics is the gentle art of getting votes from the poor and campaign contributions from the rich by promising to protect each from the other.

EDWARD BENNETT WILLIAMS (1920–88), US lawyer and political campaign organizer

The Russians are praying for a Labour victory.

DENIS HEALEY, Labour foreign affairs spokesman, opening day of the general election campaign, 1987

If you vote for Kinnock, you are voting against Christ.

DAME BARBARA CARTLAND, campaign, 1992

We will continue to launch the manifesto until we receive fair coverage.

GREEN PARTY SPOKESPERSON, at the party's second manifesto launch in three weeks, general election campaign, 1997

This union has had as much effect on wages as breaking wind has on the Richter scale.

DELEGATE to the National Union of Mineworkers' conference, 1988

Shh! Giving the Game Away

Many immigrants vote Labour because they think the labour exchanges where they sign on for unemployment benefit belong to the Labour Party.

DHARAM DUGGAL, ward chairman, Birmingham Conservative Association, c.1980

F**k off out of it if you can't observe the niceties.

ROBERT MCCARTNEY, Unionist member of the Ulster Assembly, to an English journalist not standing for the singing of the national anthem, November 1984

We must be mad, literally mad, as a nation to be permitting the annual inflow of some 50,000 dependants of immigrants . . . As I look ahead I am filled with foreboding. Like the Roman, I see the River Tiber foaming with much blood.

ENOCH POWELL, Conservative shadow defence spokesman, securing his exit from mainstream British politics, 1968

I don't really think I have ever made a mistake.

POWELL, *Any Questions?*, BBC Radio, 1982

To assume that because a party has one dominant figure it thereby benefits is not necessarily true at all . . . Nobody expects that the Prime Minister would be Prime Minister throughout the entire period of the next parliament.

JOHN BIFFEN, Leader of the House, curtailing his political career, interview on *Weekend World*, ITV, May 1986. In the same interview, he described his hopes that the Tory leadership at the next election would be 'a balanced ticket'. It sparked a furious, although indirect, response from Mrs Thatcher who let it be known through her press secretary that she regarded Biffen as a 'semi-detached' member of the government. He was sacked two days after the general election in 1987

Our human stock is threatened . . . These mothers . . . single parents from classes 4 and 5 are now producing a third of all births. If we do nothing, the nation moves towards degeneration.

SIR KEITH JOSEPH speaking to Birmingham Conservatives, October 1974. He went on to recommend 'proposals to extend birth control to these classes of people'. Reaction ended his hopes of leading his party, clearing the way for Margaret Thatcher in 1975

Shh! Giving the Game Away

Conservatism, like selfishness, is inherent in the human condition.

JOSEPH, *New Statesman*, 1975

The price of oil is not determined by the British Parliament. It is determined by some lads riding camels who do not even know how to spell national sovereignty.

LORD FEATHER, former TUC General Secretary, 1975

I will consider selling off the Crown Jewels – but I am not absolutely certain that they are the property of Her Majesty's Government.

DENIS HEALEY, Chancellor of the Exchequer, in the year Britain was bailed out by the IMF, 1976

That's OK, we milk the public for a living.

UNIDENTIFIED MP on a 'fact-finding' visit to the United States in 1991 replying off the cuff to a Hudson, Wisconsin farmer Vernon Bailey, who had introduced himself by saying, 'I milk cows for a living.' The party included Tories Roger King, James Cran and Andrew Hargreaves, and Labour's Tom Pendry and Allen McKay, but the perpetrator was not identified

I can assure you a helpful response, which your local paper may be interested in when I respond to you on the floor of the House of Commons . . .

Note by NIGEL GRIFFITHS, junior Trade and Industry minister, to a fellow Labour MP suggesting the text of a question his colleague might ask him at the next Trade and Industry question time, March 1998.

Unreconstructed wankers.

TONY BLAIR, on sections of the Scottish media, which he accused of being apologists for Old Labour, December 1996

Shh! Giving the Game Away

Even a right-wing moron in a hurry would feel completely unembarrassed to vote for us.

TONY BANKS, Labour MP for West Ham, on his modernized party, general election campaign, 1997

I have three policy announcements to underspin . . . underpin . . . the strength of our public finances.

Chancellor GORDON BROWN, Freudian slip, House of Commons, July 2000. The Blair government's image of reliance on PR 'spin' was one of its enduring features

You want spontaneity? Spontaneity is scheduled for Wednesday.

LABOUR SPIN-DOCTOR, talking to the *Observer's* Andrew Rawnsley, general election campaign, April 1997

Like a journey in which you never arrive at your destination.

GERALD CORBETT, Chief Executive of Railtrack, giving evidence to the 2000 public enquiry into the Paddington rail disaster the year before in which 31 died, choosing an unfortunate metaphor to describe his company's efforts to achieve continual improvements in rail safety

I have difficulty looking humble for extended periods of time.

HENRY KISSINGER, 1981

I am being frank about myself in this book. I tell of my first mistake on page 850.

KISSINGER, on his memoirs, *The White House Years*, 1979

The nice thing about being a celebrity is that when you bore people, they think it's their fault.

KISSINGER, 1985

I don't give a damn about protocol. I'm a swinger. Bring out the beautiful spies.

KISSINGER, reacting to seating plans for an official dinner, 1973

Shh! Giving the Game Away

He doesn't make snap decisions, but he doesn't overthink either.

NANCY REAGAN, on Ronald, 1980

I'm not doing so bad. At this point in his administration, William Henry Harrison had been dead sixty-eight days.

President BILL CLINTON, four months after his inauguration, after a series of public relations disasters in making appointments to his administration, May 1993

I'm a great believer in leaving politics when you've reached your ceiling. (*Pause*) Though, I did lower the ceiling somewhat . . .

CECIL PARKINSON, former cabinet minister, on leaving the Commons, campaign 1992

Other than when playing darts, I become confused at the mere mention of figures.

NEIL KINNOCK, then a Labour backbencher, House of Commons 1978. (The following year, he became the party's chief spokesman on education)

Had a letter from your father today about inflation . . . or deflation – or something.

Prime Minister ALEC DOUGLAS-HOME, famously economically illiterate (see p.163) to the son of a leading economist, 1964

I wonder how it is with you, Harold? If I don't have a woman for three days, I get a terrible headache.

President JOHN F. KENNEDY to Prime Minister Harold Macmillan, during working lunch on nuclear arms, 1962

Shh! Giving the Game Away

Who Governs?

TED HEATH's campaign slogan in the bitter February 1974 election held against the backdrop of a miners' strike. Heath wanted to suggest that the miners' actions threatened the norms of parliamentary democracy. As Peter Hennessy has written, Willie Whitelaw, a wise Conservative grandee, always reflected that it had been a mistake 'for a government to resort to the polls sooner than it has to and ask "Who governs?", because the country tends to reply, "We thought you were."' The public decided that Heath wasn't, and shouldn't, and elected Labour instead

It is exciting to have a real crisis on your hands when you have spent half your life dealing with humdrum issues like the environment.

MARGARET THATCHER, speech to the Scottish Conservative conference, May 1982, during the Falklands War

If I'd known that Enrique was going to be President of Bolivia, I'd have sent him to school.

A nineteenth-century Bolivian President's mother

You know, the main shortcoming of all socialist countries is that we are not clever with figures.

KIM DAL HYON, deputy Prime Minister of North Korea, asked how much the government had spent celebrating the eightieth birthday of dictator Kim Il Sung, May 1992

Canada is a country built against any common, geographic, historic or cultural sense.

PIERRE TRUDEAU, Canadian Prime Minister

Among some people in this country, for a man to express his love for his wife he must beat her sometimes.

GEORGE MASHAMBA, South African senator, addressing a parliamentary committee on education, September 1995

Shh! Giving the Game Away

The number of women aged between 15 and 50 is fixed. Because the number of birth-giving machines and devices is fixed, all we can ask is for them to do their best per head.

HAKUO YANAGISAWA, Japanese Health Minister, on his country's low birth rate, January 2007. He later said he was 'sorry to call them machines'

The committee will be composed of open-minded people who agree with me.

EDWARD McKITA, Mayor of Surrey, British Columbia, on forming a municipal art committee to censor art shows, 1976

Leave it where you got it.

TERRY TROUTT, Mayor of Romulus, Michigan, public announcement to anyone 'with a body on their hands', after complaining that his town just outside Detroit was being used as a dumping ground by murderers, 1973

Democracy has been served, the people have spoken. *(Sotto voce, to an aide)* The bastards.

Concession speech of WILLIAM WILLKIE, one of Roosevelt's opponents

I think people should elect a cat person. If you elect a dog person, you elect someone who wants to be loved. If you elect a cat person, you elect someone who wants to serve.

STEPHEN HARPER, Canadian Prime Minister, running for re-election, April 2006

The majority of those men are homosexual – perhaps not the majority – but in the USA there are already 25 per cent of them and in England and Germany it is the same. You cannot imagine it in the history of France.

EDITH CRESSON, French Prime Minister, 1991

We're in a battle that is like searching for a needle in a haystack. Sometimes to find the needle you need to burn the whole haystack.

EZER WEIZMAN, Israeli President, March 1996

Where would Christianity be if Jesus had got eight to fifteen years with time off for good behaviour?

JAMES DONOVAN, New York senator supporting capital punishment, 1978

If you've seen one city slum, you've seen them all.

SPIRO AGNEW, campaigning as Richard Nixon's vice-presidential running mate, Detroit, 1968

A tree's a tree. How many do you need to look at?

RONALD REAGAN, on plans to expand California's Redwood National Park, 1967

Seen one Redwood, you've seen 'em all.

REAGAN on ecology, quoted Melbourne Age, 1981

Why should we subsidize intellectual curiosity?

REAGAN, opposing increased education spending

The average American is just like a child.

PRESIDENT NIXON, interview with New York Times, November 1972

❖

You must remember that the Australian voter has a short memory span . . . less than 14 days in most cases.

JOHN HOWARD, Australian Prime Minister, replying to a reporter who asked what reaction the Government expected to its introduction of sales tax, 1999

❖

Shh! Giving the Game Away

What the hell would I want to go to a place like Mombasa for? ...
I just see myself in a pot of boiling water with all these natives
dancing around me.

MEL LASTMAN, Mayor of Toronto, one of the three cities bidding for the 2008
Olympic Games, to a freelance journalist declining to attend a meeting of the
Association of National Olympic Committees in Mombasa, Kenya, June 2001. A
month later the International Olympic Committee awarded the Games to Beijing

We've got to pause and ask ourselves: How much clean air do we
need?

LEE IACOCCA, chairman of the Chrysler Corporation, responding to tougher
environmental laws on vehicle emissions

Boy, they were big on crematoriums, weren't they?

GEORGE BUSH SNR, Vice-President, after visiting the death camp at Auschwitz, 1987

The B-52 has been an effective war machine. It's killed a lot of
people.

BILL YOUNG, speaking on the floor of the US House of Representatives

The B-52 has been an effective war machine which unfortunately
has killed a lot of people.

YOUNG as recorded in the Congressional Record after 'sanitizing' his speech,
1981

I want to lob one into the men's room of the Kremlin and to make
sure I hit it.

BARRY GOLDWATER, Republican presidential candidate against Lyndon Johnson, on
his ambitions for nuclear weapons, campaign 1964

I wanted to educate the American people to lose some of their
fear of the word 'nuclear'. When you say 'nuclear', all the
American people see is a mushroom cloud. But for military
purposes, it's just enough firepower to get the job done.

GOLDWATER, responding to criticism of his recklessness, 1964

Shh! Giving the Game Away

I haven't got a really first-class brain.

GOLDWATER, campaign 1964

Restraint? Why are you so concerned with saving their lives? The whole idea is to kill the bastards. At the end of the war if there are two Americans and one Russian left alive, we win.

US General THOMAS POWER, Head of Strategic Air Command, 1957-64, testimony to a Senate defense committee, February 1960

If we have to start over again with another Adam and Eve, I want them to be Americans and not Russians.

RICHARD RUSSELL, US senator for Georgia, 1968

In the Orient, life is cheap.

GENERAL WILLIAM WESTMORELAND, commander-in-chief of US troops in Vietnam, c.1967

We should declare war on North Vietnam. We could pave the whole country and put parking stripes on it, and still be home by Christmas.

RONALD REAGAN, Governor of California, 1966

If we quit Vietnam, tomorrow we'll be fighting in Hawaii and next week we'll have to fight in San Francisco.

President LYNDON JOHNSON, 1967

If only Hitler and Mussolini could have a good game of bowls once a week at Geneva, I feel that Europe would not be as troubled as it is.

CAPT R. G. BRISCOE MP, c.1937

Shh! Giving the Game Away

I often think how much easier the world would have been to manage if Herr Hitler and Signor Mussolini had been at Oxford.

LORD HALIFAX, Foreign Secretary, 1938-41

Are you aware it is private property? Why you'll be asking me to bomb Essen next.

SIR KINGSLEY WOOD, Secretary of State for Air, on plans to set fire to the Black Forest, September 1939

I read about foreign policy and studied – I know the number of continents.

GEORGE WALLACE, presidential candidate, campaigning 1968

I don't really know what a cyclotron is but I am certainly very happy Canada has one.

PIERRE TRUDEAU, Canadian Prime Minister visiting the University of British Columbia's TRIUMF cyclotron, Vancouver, 1976

I just assume somewhere in my life some knucklehead has looked at me and my brown self and said that they have given me less or denied me an opportunity. But the bottom line is, and my wife will attest to this, I am so insensitive I probably didn't notice.

GERALD REYNOLDS, December 2004, newly appointed chairman of the US Commission on Civil Rights, describing his experiences with racism in the US

Well, I never saw this before. I didn't write this speech and don't believe what I just read.

WARREN HARDING, stumbling over speech, campaign trail, 1920. (He won in a landslide)

Shh! Giving the Game Away

Something's going awry here. I mean, if I just listen to the question, I can answer whatever it is. But if it's going to be on [the script] I don't listen to the question, I just look at [the script].

President GEORGE BUSH SNR on an open microphone, inadvertently revealing that supposedly spontaneous questions from an audience, the answers to which were displayed on a teleprompter, were not coming in the order scripted by his staff, November 1991

I will learn as I go along.

WILLIAM CLARK, Ronald Reagan's choice as Deputy Secretary of State, who revealed in his nomination hearings in 1981 that he didn't know the names of the South African leaders, had not heard of the split in the British Labour Party, had 'no opinion' on the spread of nuclear weapons and relied solely on news magazines for his understanding of foreign affairs

Ireland has food and climate well matched for each other: dull.

The private observations of diplomat ROBIN BERRINGTON, Cultural Affairs and Press Officer at the American Embassy in Dublin, mistakenly included in the Embassy's publicity handout marking President Reagan's inauguration, 1981

The Irish are famous for their sense of humour. I think I shall have to rely upon it in this instance.

Berrington's boss, AMBASSADOR WILLIAM SHANNON, smoothing the ruffled feathers

Journalist: Are you not worn out by all the late nights?
Lord Halifax: Not exactly, but it spoils one's eye for the high birds.

Exchange immediately after the Munich crisis, October 1938

I am sure I will feel at home in the Bahamas . . . I love golf and they have a lot of nice golf courses and good fishing.

CHIC HECHT, President Bush Snr's nominee for US ambassador to the Bahamas, 1989. He was appointed

I saw the new Italian navy. Its boats have glass bottoms so they can see the old Italian navy.

PETER SECCHIA, Bush Snr's nominee for US ambassador to Italy, during Senate confirmation hearings, 1989. He too was approved

The tsunami was a wonderful opportunity to [in a good light] show not just the US government, but the heart of the American people, and I think it has paid great dividends for us.

CONDOLEEZZA RICE, Senate confirmation hearings on her nomination as US Secretary of State, January 2005. The Indian Ocean disaster on Boxing Day 2004 killed up to a quarter of a million people

Get some devastation in the back.

US Senator BILL FRIST to a photographer capturing his visit to tsunami-stricken Sri Lanka, January 2005

[I have spent enormous amounts of time helping the Northern Irish leaders] to get over 600 years of religious fights. And every time they make an agreement to do it, they're like a couple of drunks walking out of the bar for the last time. When they get to the swing door, they turn around and go back in.

President BILL CLINTON expressing frustration at the slow pace of the peace process, October 1999. He later apologised

If the B-2 is invisible, just announce you've built a hundred of them and don't build them.

JOHN KASICH, chairman US House Budget Committee, opposing further expenditure on the Stealth bomber designed to be invisible to radar detection, July 1995

If we [legislators] don't watch our respective tails, the people are going to be running the government.

BILL CRAVEN, Californian state senator, on the growing use of citizen-inspired state referendums

Shh! Giving the Game Away

Just going to make it up. I'm not going to talk too damn long like the rest of them.

GEORGE W. BUSH to Tony Blair before his speech to leaders at the G-8 summit in Russia, July 2006. His remark was caught by a microphone that had inadvertently been left on

Let [the French and the Germans] put their demands in such a way that Great Britain can say that she supported both sides.

RAMSAY MACDONALD, Prime Minister, minutes of the Five Power conference in Geneva on disarmament and security in Europe, December 1932

It is better to do something quite absurd for which there is a precedent than to make oneself responsible for an unprecedented act of wisdom.

ARTHUR BALFOUR, Foreign Secretary, defending the traditions of secret diplomacy in response to the call for 'open' diplomacy in American President Woodrow Wilson's Fourteen Points, House of Commons, 1918

I retract any statement that might have created the impression that any individual should be targeted for physical attack.

PETER MOKABA, South African ANC youth leader, clarifying his remarks after he had urged township residents to 'save their bullets' for President F. W. de Klerk, August 1993

If you look at, particularly African-Caribbeans 30 years ago . . . you know your head did not turn in the road if a black woman passed you because they were badly dressed, they were probably overweight and they probably had a lousy job. And you know very well if you walk down London streets now there are the most staggeringly beautiful girls of every nationality.

LORD (JEFFREY) ARCHER campaigning (unsuccessfully) for Mayor of London, August 1999. An aide optimistically explained Archer's comments: 'the whole purpose of what he was saying was that the ethnic community in London is upwardly mobile, and that's a good thing'

The chap's got no experience of government. He's hardly made a speech, or held a press conference. *(Pause)* Mind you, I suppose it's not entirely his fault.

PIK BOTHA, South African Foreign Minister, on the credentials for leadership of the then still jailed Nelson Mandela, reported by David Steel MP during visit, 1986

What a mighty man he turns out to be! He raped ten women – I would never have expected this from him. He surprised us all – we all envy him.

Russian President VLADIMIR PUTIN to visiting Israeli Prime Minister Ehud Olmert on Israel's President, Moshe Katsav, who was being investigated on rape charges, October 2006

In Israel, in order to be realistic, you have to believe in miracles.

DAVID BEN-GURION, first Prime Minister of Israel

Marijuana smokers, drug addicts, long-hairs, homosexuals and unionists.

GENERAL PINOCHET, former President of Chile, describing the West German army, 1990. He later issued an apology saying that his comments 'were never meant to offend the army'

If you want to steal, steal a little cleverly, in a nice way. If you steal so much as to become rich overnight, you will be caught.

MOBUTU SESE SEKO, President of Zaire, anti-corruption speech, 1976. His own fortune plundered from his country is estimated at $5 billion

Show me just what Muhammad brought that was new, and there you will find things only evil and inhuman, such as his command to spread by the sword the faith he preached.

Pope BENEDICT XVI, quoting the 14th century Byzantine Emperor Manuel II Paleologus during a lecture in Germany, September 2006

Shh! Giving the Game Away

The Holy Father is very sorry that some passages of his speech may have sounded offensive to the sensibilities of Muslim believers.

Vatican Secretary of State, TARCISIO BERTONE, reading a statement of apology after the Pope's remarks sparked a worldwide furore.

From 20,000 feet in the air, on the way to Paris.

Australian Prime Minister PAUL KEATING, when asked the best way to see Darwin, the Northern Territory capital, quoted 1996

In terms of the unemployed . . . don't feel particularly bad for many of these people. They don't feel bad about it themselves, as long as they're receiving generous social assistance and unemployment insurance.

STEPHEN HARPER, future Canadian Prime Minister, June 1997

I was thinking of you last night, Helmut, because I was watching the sumo wrestling on television.

President BILL CLINTON, greeting Germany's Chancellor Kohl, at NATO summit, Brussels, January 1994

We have that trouble in our family, too.

PRINCE PHILIP, during a visit to Australia, 1954, being introduced to a married couple. The husband had introduced them by saying, 'My wife's a doctor of philosophy. She is much more important than me.'

Wasn't it too bad you sent your royal family to the guillotine?

PRINCE PHILIP, to the French Minister of the Interior, on the tumultuous reception he and Queen Elizabeth received from Parisian crowds during their visit, April 1957

I never see any home cooking – all I get is fancy stuff.

PRINCE PHILIP, 1962

Shh! Giving the Game Away

Are you sure you want to go through with this?

PRINCE PHILIP, aside to new Prime Minister Jomo Kenyatta during the Kenya independence ceremony in 1963, inadvertently picked up by microphones and broadcast to the watching crowd

The monarchy exists not for its own benefit, but for that of the country. We don't come here for our health. We can think of better ways of enjoying ourselves.

PRINCE PHILIP, addressing audience in Ottawa, royal visit to Canada

What a po-faced lot these Dutch are.

PRINCE PHILIP, during motorcade drive on visit to Amsterdam, 1968

Don't stay here too long or you'll go back with slitty eyes.

PRINCE PHILIP, to British students in Peking, 1986

Manchester is not such a nice place.

QUEEN ELIZABETH, to a student in St Petersburg, 1994

A few years ago everybody was saying we must have more leisure, everybody is working too much. Now that everybody has got so much leisure – it may be involuntary, but they have got it – they are now complaining they are unemployed. People do not seem to be able to make up their minds, do they?

PRINCE PHILIP, 1981

I'm prepared to take advice on leisure from Prince Philip. He's a world expert on leisure. He's been practising for most of his adult life.

NEIL KINNOCK

The grouse are in no danger from those who shoot grouse.

PRINCE PHILIP, on field sports, 1988

Shh! Giving the Game Away

I don't think a prostitute is more moral than a wife, but they are doing the same thing.

PRINCE PHILIP, 1988

How do you keep the natives off the booze long enough to get them past the test?

PRINCE PHILIP, to a driving instructor during a visit to Oban, 1995

If a cricketer suddenly decided to go into a school and batter a lot of people to death with a cricket bat – which he could do very easily – are you going to ban cricket bats?

PRINCE PHILIP, responding to a question about gun control, 1996, after a gunman had killed 16 children and their teacher at a school in Dunblane, Scotland

It looks as though it was put in by an Indian.

PRINCE PHILIP, pointing out a poorly maintained fuse box in a factory he was visiting, Edinburgh, August 1999

A pissometer?

PRINCE PHILIP, at the top of his voice, visiting a winery in New South Wales, being shown a piezometer, a device measuring water depth in soil, March 2000

But will they ever produce enough electricity to make the turbines go round?

PRINCE PHILIP, showing a less than perfect grasp of the principles of wind power generation, during a visit to the Royal Society, May 2001

You look as if you're ready for bed.

PRINCE PHILIP to a berobed Emeka Anyaoku, the Nigerian Secretary-General of the Commonwealth

Do you still throw spears at each other?

PRINCE PHILIP to an aboriginal businessman during a visit to Queensland, March 2002

It's like being in the Scouts.

PRINCE PHILIP during a traditional aboriginal 'making fire' welcoming ceremony, same visit, same day

Shh! Giving the Game Away

Do you know they're now producing eating dogs for the anorexics?

PRINCE PHILIP greeting a blind, wheelchair-bound woman and guide dog, Bath, May 2002

So you can write then?

PRINCE PHILIP, on a visit to Romford, Essex, March 2003, greeting 14-year-old George Barlow who had invited him to visit the town

If it has got four legs and it is not a chair, if it has got two wings and flies but is not an aeroplane, and if it swims and is not a submarine, the Chinese will eat it.

PRINCE PHILIP

I thought Eastern women just sit around smoking pipes and eating sweets all day.

PRINCE PHILIP meeting a troupe of belly dancers, Swansea, March 2008

What is it that makes everyone think they are qualified to do things far beyond their technical capabilities? People think they can all be pop stars, high-court judges, brilliant TV personalities or infinitely more competent heads of state without ever putting in the necessary work or having natural ability.

PRINCE CHARLES, describing an employee who had charged the royal household with sex discrimination and unfair dismissal, November 2004

It makes me look so old, but then I suppose I am old.

QUEEN ELIZABETH, on newly designed £5 notes which showed her with a double chin, wrinkles and bags under her eyes, June 1990

I didn't realise the whole family were here.

QUEEN ELIZABETH, reportedly, at the Chelsea flower show 2001 while viewing a display of creepers, spiders and strangely shaped foreign vegetables

The monarchy is the oldest profession in the world.

PRINCE CHARLES, c.1980 (attrib.)

83

Just call me Madam.

Betty Boothroyd, first woman Deputy Speaker of the Commons, advising MPs how to address her, 1987

This woman is headstrong, obstinate and dangerously self-opinionated.

Report by Personnel Office at ICI, rejecting the 22-year-old Margaret Roberts (soon-to-be Thatcher) as a possible employee, 1948

They put me through to the Prime Minister. He then obviously recognized that there was a mistake and somebody pulled the plug. I was a Minister of State for eight seconds.

Brian Donohoe, newly elected Labour MP, after being wrongly connected by Tony Blair's officials. Blair's real choice was Lord (Bernard) Donoughue

That's enough health, I need a fag.

Charles Kennedy, Liberal Democrat spokesman, after posing at a Glasgow supermarket to promote healthy food, June 1999

We have just begun to fight. And we're going to fight and fight and fight. . . . Not only are we going to New Hampshire. We're going to South Carolina and Oklahoma and Arizona and North Dakota and New Mexico. We're going to California and Texas and New York. And we're going to South Dakota and Oregon and Washington . . . We will not quit, now or ever.

US presidential hopeful Howard Dean self-destructing in a speech to supporters in Iowa after a surprise poor showing early in the primary elections, January 2004. His words were bawled out with increasing ferocity, a newspaper account reporting: 'In a furious climax, having exhausted all recognisable vowels and consonants, he simply roared at the microphone in his hand like a child imitating a Tyrannosaurus rex.' The moment quickly became celebrated as Dean's 'I have a scream' speech. He quit the campaign three weeks later

Shh! Giving the Game Away

SITUATIONS: DOMESTIC. Cheerful, energetic and loving nanny/
mother's help [who could] enjoy the relaxed and happy life in our
family with Amy, 3, Hanna, 5, Lizzi, 10, and Nicky, 12.

Advertisement placed in *The Lady* magazine for June 1984 by a lady who turned
out to be Councillor MRS MARGARET HODGE, then Leader of the red-flag-flying
and Lenin's-bust-displaying Islington Borough Council and now Labour
frontbencher and MP for Barking. The advertisement added that a cleaner was
also employed and there were 'plenty of local nannies'

But Gordon? He can't defeat Cameron.

TONY BLAIR on his successor Gordon Brown's electoral chances against
Conservative leader, David Cameron, according to the memoirs of Blair
confidante, Lord Levy, April 2008. In public, Blair denied the quote

If you don't have anything nice to say – let's hear it.

Said to be the motto of the WASHINGTON PRESS CORPS

85

4

Er . . .

If Only They'd Known

New facts can be inconvenient and the march of history can be straight over one's blithest assumptions. Events can leave politicians floundering, but the statesman who never said anything the passage of time left him regretting, never said anything. Those quoted below were bolder, worse luck. 'If I knew then what I know now . . .'

The French people are incapable of regicide.

LOUIS XVI OF FRANCE, four years before he was guillotined, 1789

A difficult and hardly comprehensible work which few would read and still fewer understand.

RUSSIAN OFFICIAL CENSOR, 1881, passing Marx's *Das Kapital* for translation into Russian, quoted by David McLellan, *Karl Marx: The Legacy*, 1983

England is at last ripe for revolution.

LEON TROTSKY, 1925

[Income tax] is not well adapted for a permanent portion of [the] fiscal system . . . on 5 April 1860, the income tax will expire.

Chancellor of the Exchequer WILLIAM GLADSTONE, first budget speech April 1853, announcing plans to phase income tax out over seven years. He was Chancellor again when 1860 came: income tax was not abolished; on the contrary, he raised rates by a penny

He falls instantly in and out of love. His present attachment will follow the course of all the others.

WINSTON CHURCHILL, on Edward VII's relationship with Mrs Simpson, 1936

. . . A party of great vested interests . . . corruption at home, aggression to cover up abroad . . . sentiment by the bucket-load, patriotism by the imperial pint.

CHURCHILL speaking on the Tories while a Liberal MP

The men who win wars are the men with burning hearts and cool heads . . . It is because I see that combination present in the Prime Minister that I would rather trust him to lead us to victory than any other man.

HENRY BROOKE, consigning himself to backbench obscurity by supporting Neville Chamberlain in the famous Commons debate of 1940 which led to Chamberlain's resignation and Churchill's premiership. Brooke had to wait fourteen years for his first ministerial post; he rose to be Home Secretary, 1962–4

No evidence has been found to show that [Kim Philby] was responsible for warning Burgess or Maclean. While in government service he carried out his duties ably and conscientiously. I have no reason to conclude that Mr Philby has at any time betrayed the interests of this country, or to identify him with the so-called 'third man', if, indeed, there was one.

HAROLD MACMILLAN, then Foreign Secretary, House of Commons debate on the defection of Soviet spies Burgess and Maclean, November 1955

[The security services] are now aware . . . that he [Philby] worked for the Soviet authorities before 1946 and that in 1951 he in fact warned Maclean through Burgess that the security services were about to take action against him.

EDWARD HEATH, Lord Privy Seal, statement to the House of Commons, July 1963

Er . . . If Only They'd Known

Our problem at the moment is a problem of success.

HEATH, a month and a half before the three-day week, November 1973

I am not proposing to seek your votes because there is blue sky ahead today.

JAMES CALLAGHAN, Prime Minister, broadcast to the nation, announcing his decision not to call a general election, September 1978. The Winter of Discontent which followed put paid to his chances of re-election when the election did come the following May

The forthcoming general election will be the most open battle in recent political history.

ROY HATTERSLEY, Labour shadow home affairs spokesman, March 1983. The election in June resulted in a 144 seat Conservative majority, the biggest since 1945. By contrast, Labour won the lowest ever share of the vote by a principal party of opposition.

In less than two years there will be a Labour government in Britain. I waste no time in justifying that assertion.

HATTERSLEY, September 1986

From here on it's downhill all the way.

Unwittingly prophetic opening of CHARLES KENNEDY'S acceptance speech on becoming Liberal Democrat leader, August 1999. After long battles with alcohol-related problems, taunting by critics for his love of chat show appearances on television and questioning of his work effort (he was dubbed 'inaction man' in contrast to his ex-Marines predecessor Paddy Ashdown) he resigned in 2006

In another five years I will have been in eleven and a half years, then someone else will carry the torch.

MARGARET THATCHER, quoted in the *Observer*, 17 November 1985. Exactly five years to the week later, she was indeed ousted by the Conservative Party

Er . . . If Only They'd Known

We will govern as we have campaigned – strongly, positively, looking to the future. The contrast with the Tories could not be more sharp. They are a spent force.

NEIL KINNOCK, party election rally, Sheffield, 1992

We're all right. We're all right. We're all right. We're all right.

KINNOCK, Sheffield, 1992, days before losing

Go back to your constituencies and prepare for government!

DAVID STEEL, Liberal leader to Liberal Party conference, 1985

I sense that the British electorate is now itching to break out once and for all from the discredited strait-jacket of the past.

STEEL, general election, June 1987. The itch was contained

Only some ghastly, dehumanised moron would want to get rid of the Routemaster.

KEN LIVINGSTONE, Mayor of London and in charge of transport for the city, speaking in 2001 about its iconic red bus; by December 2005 he had had them all phased out

Made in South Africa.

STEPHEN BYERS, Trade and Industry Secretary, ambushed into identifying the origin of his suit when hosting a meeting intended to promote Britain's ailing textile industry, June 2000. A press report, describing his being cajoled into removing his jacket and searching for the label, recorded that 'there was a split-second hesitation before he revealed its origins'

The Chancellor's position is unassailable.

THATCHER endorsing Nigel Lawson, shortly before she began to assail it herself by taking separate economic advice from her personal adviser Sir Alan Walters. Lawson resigned in protest in 1989 after she refused his ultimatum to dismiss Walters

Rather easygoing in Maths.

Extract from school report of former Chancellor of the Exchequer, Kenneth Clarke

He will never get to the top in English politics, for all his wonderful gifts; to speak with the tongue of men and angels, and to spend laborious days and nights in administration is not good if a man does not inspire trust.

HERBERT ASQUITH, on Winston Churchill

His style . . . is not very literary, and he lacks force.

Daily News, reporting Winston Churchill's maiden speech in the House of Commons, February 1901

If paternity leave was granted, it would result in a direct incitement to a population explosion.

Conservative MP IAN GOW, 1979

By the end of 1991, it is not unreasonable to suppose that motoring will become an occupation indulged in by the super-rich, just as it was in the early 1920s.

LORD TANLAW, Liberal peer, 1977

If cars continue to be made at the same rate as now and with increasing cheapness, there will soon be no pedestrians left.

LESLIE HORE-BELISHA, Minister of Transport, 1935

Personally, I do not believe that we shall have greater armaments in the future than we have had in the past. On the contrary, I believe there will be a gradual diminution in this respect.

WILLIAM WATSON MP, House of Commons, 1924

Er . . . If Only They'd Known

[The atomic bomb] is the biggest fool thing we have ever done . . . The bomb will never go off – and I speak as an expert in explosives.

ADMIRAL WILLIAM LEAHY, US chief of staff advising President Truman, 1945

Atomic energy might be as good as our present-day explosives, but it is unlikely to produce anything very much more dangerous.

WINSTON CHURCHILL, 1939

The Olympic movement appears as a ray of sunshine through the clouds of racial animosity, religious bigotry and political chicanery.

AVERY BRUNDAGE, President of the International Olympic Committee, 1972, before the Munich massacre, the Montreal games which were boycotted by the Africans, the Moscow games which were boycotted by the West, and the Los Angeles games which were boycotted by the Eastern bloc

It could no more lose money than I could have a baby.

JEAN DRAPEAU, Mayor of Montreal, on his city hosting the 1976 Olympics, January 1973. The games left Montreal with a debt of over $1 billion

There will be one million AIDS cases in Britain by the end of 1991.

WORLD HEALTH ORGANIZATION REPORT, July 1989. By March 1994 there had been just 9,000 cases.

Within a decade we will build a world party of socialist revolution [and become] the decisive force on the planet.

MILITANT TENDENCY publicity, 1981

❖

We in America today are nearer to the final triumph over poverty than ever before in the history of any land . . . We shall soon with the help of God be in sight of the day when poverty will be banished from this nation.

HERBERT HOOVER, soon-to-be President, accepting the Republican nomination, 1928, twelve months before the Great Crash

Er . . . If Only They'd Known

No Congress of the United States ever assembled, on surveying the state of the Union, has met with a more pleasing prospect than that which appears at the present time.

CALVIN COOLIDGE, December 1928

The government's business is in sound condition.

ANDREW MELLON, US Secretary of the Treasury, five weeks after the crash, December 1929

I see nothing . . . in the present situation that is either menacing or warrants pessimism.

MELLON, January 1930

The worst effect of the crash upon unemployment will have been passed during the next sixty days.

PRESIDENT HOOVER, March 1930. Unemployment was then some three million. It reached thirteen million, at the end of 1932, before recovery began

We are likely to find the country as a whole enjoying its wonted state of prosperity. Business will be normal in two months.

ROBERT LAMONT, Secretary of Commerce, March 1930

Normal conditions should be restored in two or three months.

LAMONT, May 1930

The worst is over without a doubt.

JAMES DAVIS, US Agriculture Secretary, six months into the Great Depression, June 1930

Courage and resource are already swinging us back on the road to recovery.

DAVIS, six weeks later

Er . . . If Only They'd Known

We have hit bottom and are on the upswing.

DAVIS, September 1930

The decline in business has substantially if not wholly ceased.

ROBERT LAMONT, September 1930

There undoubtedly will be an appreciable decrease in the number of unemployed by mid-summer.

LAMONT, March 1931

I have been singing in the bath.

British chancellor NORMAN LAMONT, at the Munich G7 economic summit, July 1992, two months before he withdrew Britain from the European Exchange Rate Mechanism

In all likelihood, world inflation is over.

PER JACOBSSON, managing director of the International Monetary Fund, 1959

It is doubtful . . . if German production would be such as to challenge our strong position in most markets outside Europe.

Conclusion of REPORT ON BRITAIN'S EXPORT OUTLOOK, Board of Trade, 1950

You can forget about OPEC [the organization of oil-producing countries]. They will never amount to a row of beans.

LORD ROBENS, Chairman of the National Coal Board 1961–71, quoting the advice he received from a senior Ministry of Power official in 1967

We are facing a new era. Labour can deliver the goods.

CLEMENT ATTLEE, on becoming Prime Minister, 1945

We have turned our backs on the economics of scarcity.

HERBERT MORRISON, deputy Prime Minister, Labour Party conference, 1946

I have no easy words for the nation. I cannot say when we shall emerge into easier times.

CLEMENT ATTLEE, introducing emergency austerity measures during the economic crisis, 1947

I sum up the prospects for 1967 in three short sentences. We are back on course. The ship is picking up speed. The economy is moving. Every seaman knows the command at such a moment, 'Steady as she goes.'

JAMES CALLAGHAN, Chancellor of the Exchequer, Budget speech, March 1967. By the autumn, he had to recommend devaluation of the pound by 14 per cent

Far from being a vote loser, with your help it will be a vote winner and launch us on our fourth term.

MICHAEL PORTILLO, local government minister, defending the poll tax, Conservative Party conference, October 1990

It is in everyone's interests to reduce broken families and the number of single parents; I have seen from my constituency the consequences of marital breakdown.

Conservative minister TIM YEO, before the story of his mistress and child were revealed in 1994

Married with a family and therefore understands the needs of families. He is a man of integrity who believes in traditional moral values, discipline, and effective law and order.

Election address by Conservative MP DAVID ASHBY, 1992. He later unsuccessfully sued the *Sunday Times* for suggesting that he was a closet homosexual

Family.

One of the 'recreations' listed by ROD RICHARDS in parliamentary biographical directory. He resigned in 1996 after allegations of an extramarital affair

Er . . . If Only They'd Known

The day hasn't yet arrived when an MP can be unseated by a gossip columnist.

MAUREEN COLQUHOUN MP after being outed as a lesbian by Nigel Dempster in 1977. The day soon did. She lost her seat at the election in 1979

I see no reason why the mass of British business should find itself short of money in the coming year . . . Business is in a uniquely favourable position today.

DENIS HEALEY, Chancellor of the Exchequer, House of Commons, April 1974

There's a collapse of business confidence in Britain . . .

HEALEY, September 1974

By the end of next year, we shall be on our way to that so-called economic miracle we need.

HEALEY, Budget broadcast, April 1976

If we can keep our heads – and our nerve – the long-awaited economic miracle is in our grasp.

HEALEY, July 1976

What I have always said is that no government can produce an economic miracle.

HEALEY, December 1976

Economic forecasts are no better than the long-range weather forecasts.

HEALEY, looking back on his chancellorship of 1974–9

A monstrous folly which we should divest ourselves of as soon as possible.

PADDY ASHDOWN, freshly elected Liberal MP, on Britain's nuclear deterrent, July 1984

Er . . . If Only They'd Known

I never took the view that this country did not need an independent deterrent.

PADDY ASHDOWN, Liberal Democrat party leader, BBC interview, just before the April 1992 general election

Even more important than tanks and guns was the steadfast political will of the people.

Prime Minister TONY BLAIR, brochure marking the 50th anniversary of NATO, 1999. As a member of the Campaign for Nuclear Disarmament's parliamentary group in the early 1980s, Blair advocated Britain's withdrawal from NATO

There will be few politicians standing for election next time on a platform advocating 'free markets'.

BLAIR, then Labour front-bench spokesman on economic affairs, on the stock market crash, October 1987

I snuck on the plane, and we were literally about to take off when the stewardess came up to me and said: 'I don't think I actually saw your boarding pass.'

BLAIR, December 1996, recollecting his attempt, aged 14, to flee public school by running away and boarding a plane at Newcastle airport 'for the Bahamas'. His father commented 'He only got as far as the airport. He never got on the plane. It was not possible. He never had a passport.' A spokeswoman for Newcastle airport said, 'In all our 61-year history, we have never had any flights to the Bahamas from here'

Indeed she was probably, at the stage she became a company director, one of a small number of women who were company directors.

GORDON BROWN, shadow Chancellor, November 1996, describing his mother's business background during an interview designed to show that 'business is in my blood'. Mrs Brown denied it: 'I don't know why Gordon is saying all this. It's all a bit embarrassing. I was not a working director at all'

Er . . . If Only They'd Known

I have very few warm words about Tony Blair. I look and listen to this man and don't feel encouraged. It's all rather dauntingly convincing in its glib, Pepsident-way: there is a sort of orthodontic gleam to the man . . . I am glumly reconciled to the fact that this man will take over.

Excerpts from interview with JONATHAN MILLER, theatrical director, released by Labour press office in February 1996 to capitalize on a Conservative press office slip-up which had wrongly cited Miller as a supporter of the House of Lords. The interview contained Miller's opposition to the Upper House, but the spin doctors failed to spot these other answers

There is no evidence at all of price increases stored up in the pipeline.

SHIRLEY WILLIAMS, Prices and Consumer Protection Secretary, three days before polling day, October 1974. Inflation would continue to rise until it reached a record 26.9 per cent in the following August.

To paraphrase Winston Churchill, I did not take the oath I have just taken with the intention of presiding over the dissolution of the world's strongest economy.

RONALD REAGAN, inaugural presidential address, January 1981. Under his leadership, America's trade deficit multiplied six-fold, while the national debt tripled. The $2 *trillion* he added to the debt was more than all his predecessors combined

Sometimes I've heard it said that Conservatives have been associated with unemployment. That's absolutely wrong. We'd have been drummed out of office if we'd had this level of unemployment.

MARGARET THATCHER, leader of the Opposition, party political broadcast, May 1977. Unemployment was then 1.3 million. It would exceed three million during her prime ministership, and would never be less than 1.3 million

Er . . . If Only They'd Known

I have never been prouder to be a citizen of Belfast than at this time. Protestant and Catholic, rich and poor, are maintaining a standard of community stability that compares with anything that has ever been recorded in the annals of Europe.

DAVID BLEAKLEY, Northern Ireland Minister of Community Relations, speech to the 1972 annual Ulster Institute of the Deaf, which was then interrupted by the sound of three car bomb explosions outside the hall

Nobody need be worried about BSE in this country or anywhere else.

JOHN GUMMER, Agriculture Minister, House of Commons, 1990

There is continued downturn in incidence of BSE.

ANGELA BROWNING, junior agriculture minister, House of Commons, May 1995. By May 1996, BSE had affected 160,000 cattle on more than 30,000 farms

Beef is perfectly safe and a good product.

DOUGLAS HOGG, Agriculture Minister, House of Commons, November 1995

Our policy has been one of total transparency. There is no way we can conceal evidence even if we wanted to.

SIR KENNETH CALMAN, Government Chief Medical Officer, December 1995

Even if science was wrong on that subject, we've removed from the human food chain the organs that could conceivably be linked to a transmission.

STEPHEN DORRELL, Health Secretary, December 1995

I would like to make a statement about the latest advice which the government has received from the Spongiform Encephalopathy Advisory Committee . . . [it] has identified a previously unrecognized and consistent disease pattern . . . the Committee have concluded that the most likely explanation at present is that these cases are linked to exposure to BSE.

DORRELL, House of Commons, May 1996

Er . . . If Only They'd Known

There is no need . . . to revise . . . advice on the safety of milk.

DORRELL, House of Commons, same day

The government has always assumed that maternal transmission [via milk] was theoretically possible.

MINISTRY OF AGRICULTURE PRESS RELEASE, August 1996

We are confident that by the end of September we will have brought this under control.

TONY BLAIR on the challenge of street crime, April 2002

The cumulative effects of the economic and financial sanctions might well bring the rebellion to an end within a matter of weeks rather than months.

HAROLD WILSON on Rhodesia crisis, January 1966, two months after the unilateral declaration of independence. (It took another fourteen years)

At all times I will be strong in purpose, steadfast in will, resolute in action.

GORDON BROWN, speech on becoming Prime Minister, June 2007. Having stoked up media speculation during the summer of an autumn election, Brown decided in October to cancel the plans. From then on, the 'dither' tag stuck. According to the *Guardian*, by December 2007, Brown had notched up 50 reviews, inquiries, consultations and policy rethinks, branded by critics as substitutes for action. Nine months in, comedian Rory Bremner summed up the disappointment of the Brown takeover: 'It's like having an uncle who's been building something in the shed for 10 years: you look through the window and there's nothing there.' Government peer Lord Desai concluded 'Gordon Brown was put on Earth to remind people how good Tony Blair was.'

I made my decision on this basis: I wanted more time to set out my vision for the future of the country without a summer dealing with issues from foot and mouth, to floods, to terrorism, to economic and financial crisis.

BROWN explaining his decision not to call an autumn election, Downing Street press conference, 8 October 2007. In the year that followed, he had more, much more, of the same

Er ... If Only They'd Known

David Cameron: Can I congratulate the Prime Minister on making absolutely the right decision with regard to the Dalai Lama? It is a difficult decision, but it would not have been made any better by delaying it, and I congratulate him on doing the right thing.
The Prime Minister: We make the right decisions at all times.

GORDON BROWN setting up hostages to fortune, House of Commons, 19 March 2008

The tax cuts I have made today are tax cuts to encourage work and make work pay, tax cuts for a purpose. They help all middle and lower-income families. They are tax cuts for the many ... a better deal for work, a better deal for the family.

GORDON BROWN, as Chancellor of the Exchequer, introducing the 10p income tax rate, Budget speech, March 1999

Everybody now agrees that the 10p rate is not the best way to tackle poverty.

GORDON BROWN, House of Commons, April 2008. Brown had announced the abolition of the 10p rate a year before, arguing the need for 'more focused ways of incentivising work and directly supporting children.' A self-inflicted row erupted when the measure came into effect when it became clear that thousands of poorer tax payers had ended up financially worse off overall

I give Castro a year. No longer.

FULGENCIO BATISTA, ousted Cuban dictator, 1959

The regime will not last long. It is in a period of terrible decadence. It is not a question of days, but perhaps a year, not more than that.

ROMEL IGLESIAS GONZALEZ, head of Cuba's government-run radio, defecting to the United States, March 1991

Stick a fork in him, he's done.

JAMES BAKER, former US Secretary of State, predicting the imminent collapse of Fidel Castro's regime in Cuba after Castro had announced plans for economic reforms, March 1994

Er . . . If Only They'd Known

I believe he [Stalin] is truly representative of the heart and soul of Russia; and I believe that we are going to get along very well with him and the Russian people.

FRANKLIN ROOSEVELT, Christmas fireside chat radio broadcast 1943, after the Big Power war-time conferences at Teheran and Cairo

[Stalin has] something else in him besides this revolutionist Bolshevist thing . . . I think that something [has] entered into his nature of the way in which a Christian gentleman should behave.

ROOSEVELT to his Cabinet, on his return from the Yalta conference, 1945. He ascribed the special quality as having come from Stalin's early education for the priesthood

Every year humanity takes a step towards Communism. Maybe not you, but at all events your grandson will surely be a Communist.

NIKITA KHRUSHCHEV, to Sir William Hayter, British ambassador to Moscow, June 1956

Whether you like it or not, history is on our side. We will bury you.

KHRUSHCHEV, to western diplomats, Moscow, November 1956

We occupy second place in the world. We have left England behind . . . We have also left France behind, and comrades, there is only America left. She can be compared to a worn-out runner. United States scientists have reported that Russia will overtake America in 1970. They are quite right. That is our date.

KHRUSHCHEV, 1959

The Communist Party has no God-given right to rule.

MIKHAIL GORBACHEV, 1989

Workers of the world – we apologize.

Banner carried by reformist protestors in Moscow during a parade to commemorate the seventy-second anniversary of the Bolshevik revolution, 1989

Er . . . If Only They'd Known

It would have been better if the experiment had been conducted in some small country to make it clear that it was a Utopian idea.

BORIS YELTSIN, on Communism, September 1991

The American disputes are settled and there is nothing to interrupt the peace and prosperity of the nation.

LORD NORTH, Prime Minister, after removing all taxes (except on tea) imposed on the American colonies, April 1771

[There is] the fairest prospect of the continuance of peace that I have known in my lifetime.

LORD NORTH, presenting his budget, May 1772. (The American War of Independence was less than three years away)

Four or five frigates will do the business without any military force.

LORD NORTH, on dealing with the rebellious American colonies, one year before the outbreak of war, House of Commons, 1774

So very contemptible is the rebel force now in all parts, and so vast is our superiority everywhere, that no resistance on their [the Americans'] part is to be apprehended that can materially obstruct the progress of the King's army in the speedy suppression of the rebellion.

LORD GEORGE GERMAIN, Secretary of State for the Colonies, 1781

The President's silly remarks.

UNIDENTIFIED US NEWSPAPER on Lincoln's Gettysburg Address, 1863, seen by one modern historian as 'the best short speech since the Sermon on the Mount'

Anything more dull and commonplace it wouldn't be easy to reproduce.

THE TIMES (London), on the Address, 1863

He is not known except as a slang-whanging stump speaker of which all parties are ashamed.

ALBANY ATLAS AND ARGUS, on Abraham Lincoln's selection as Republican candidate, 1860 election

Er . . . If Only They'd Known

The conduct of the Republican Party in this nomination is a remarkable indication of the small intellect, growing smaller . . . they take up a fourth-rate lecturer, who cannot speak good grammar, and who . . . delivers hackneyed, illiterate compositions.

NEW YORK HERALD on Lincoln

A horrid-looking wretch he is, sooty and scoundrelly in aspect, a cross between the nutmeg dealer, the horse swapper, and the night man, a creature fit evidently for petty treason, small stratagems and all sorts of spoils.

CHARLESTON MERCURY on Lincoln

Lincoln is the leanest, lankest, most ungainly mass of legs and arms and hatchet face ever strung on a single frame. He has most unwarrantably abused the privilege, which all politicians have, of being ugly.

HOUSTON TELEGRAPH

Tell us he resembles Jackson,
Save he wears a larger boot,
And is broader 'cross the shoulders
And is taller by a foot.

Any lie we'll swallow –
Swallow any kind of mixture;
But O don't, we beg and pray you
Don't for land's sake, show his picture.

Democratic Party campaign ballad, 1860 election

It's a kangaroo ticket – stronger in the hindquarters than in the front.

Texan Democrat on the relative merits of the party's nomination of New York Governor Franklin Roosevelt for President and the more experienced congressman, John Garner, Speaker of the House, 1932

Here was a great convention . . . nominating the weakest candidate before it.

H. L. MENCKEN, editor, the *American Mercury* of Roosevelt's nomination

Er . . . If Only They'd Known

. . . an amiable boy scout.

WALTER LIPPMANN, celebrated American political commentator, on Roosevelt

The grass will grow in the streets of 100 cities.

HERBERT HOOVER, incumbent President, on prospects if his opponent Franklin
Roosevelt won the election, campaign, 1932

They can beat him [Roosevelt] with a Chinaman.

H. L. MENCKEN, doyen of American political commentators, predicting the
outcome of the 1936 election – which Roosevelt won by what still remains the
largest ever margin of electoral college votes, 523–8

The main question is whether Governor Dewey will win by a fair
margin or by a landslide.

NEW YORK SUN, a month before polling, October 1948

President Truman appears to be the only American who doesn't
think Thomas E. Dewey is going to be elected barring a political
earthquake.

NEW YORK DAILY NEWS, two weeks before polling, October 1948

It is a godsend to this country and to the world at large that Harry
Truman will get his dismissal notice next Tuesday.

SAN FRANCISCO CHRONICLE, a week before polling, October 1948

Truman put up a courageous fight, but . . . he cannot possibly win.

BALTIMORE SUN, eve of polling, November 1948

DEWEY DEFEATS TRUMAN

CHICAGO DAILY TRIBUNE headline, day after polling, still getting the outcome of
the 1948 presidential election wrong

This is not a landslide country.

TONY BLAIR, general election campaign, April 1997

Er . . . If Only They'd Known

DRY LAND, BUT PROBABLY NOT A LANDSLIDE
New Statesman headline predicting result, 25 April 1997

HISTORIC LANDSLIDE COLLECTOR'S EDITION
New Statesman headline, after result, 6 May 1997

We have the happiest Africans in the world.
Ian Smith, Rhodesian Prime Minister, November 1971

There are going to be no dramatic changes in Rhodesia.
Smith, January 1975

I don't believe in black majority rule in Rhodesia . . . not in a thousand years.
Smith, March 1976

We live in a world of rapid change, and if we are to survive in such a world we must be prepared to subject ourselves to change.
Smith, September 1976

If I have anything to do with it, any handover of power to the Patriotic Front will not take place.
Smith, July 1977

I have got to admit that things haven't gone quite the way I wanted.
Smith, June 1979

Mugabe is a Marxist terrorist . . . an Apostle of Satan.
Ian Smith, before Mugabe's takeover in Rhodesia/Zimbabwe

He's sober and responsible. He's a pragmatist and his government will probably be the best in Africa.
Smith, after Mugabe's takeover

❖

Er . . . If Only They'd Known

We can now look forward with something like confidence to the time when war between civilized nations will be considered as antiquated as a duel.

GEORGE PEABODY GOOCH, 1906–10, shortly after losing his seat in the House of Commons, in *History of Our Time* (1911)

Happily there seems to be no reason why we should be anything but spectators [of the approaching war].

HERBERT ASQUITH, Prime Minister, July 1914

You will be home before the leaves have fallen from the trees.

KAISER WILHELM II of Germany, addressing troops leaving for the Western Front, August 1914

The League of Nations grows in moral courage. Its frown will soon be more dreaded than a nation's arms, and when that happens you and I shall have security and peace.

RAMSAY MACDONALD, Prime Minister, on the ill-fated League which proved toothless and powerless in the 1930s. Lord Mayor's banquet speech, November 1929

For what? A war with Japan! But why should there be a war with Japan? I do not believe there is the slightest chance of it in our lifetime.

WINSTON CHURCHILL, Chancellor of the Exchequer, to Prime Minister Stanley Baldwin, opposing the Admiralty's plans for rearming the navy, December 1924

When I agreed in principle to the base at Singapore, I had never imagined that that decision would be used as a peg on which to hang far-reaching schemes of alarmist policy and consequential armament. I do not believe there is any danger to be apprehended from Japan.

CHURCHILL, reiterating his opposition to British naval strengthening in the Far East, Committee of Imperial Defence, July 1926

Er . . . If Only They'd Known

I am going to say something to you which is very unfashionable – a word of sympathy for Japan. I do not think the League of Nations would be well advised to have a quarrel with Japan.

CHURCHILL, on Japan's conquest of Manchuria, House of Commons, February 1933

So great a man . . . so wise a ruler.

CHURCHILL on Mussolini, September 1935

If I had been an Italian, I should have been on Mussolini's side fifteen years ago.

CHURCHILL, July 1937

He is a queer fellow who will never become Chancellor. The best he can hope for is to head the Postal Department.

PAUL VON HINDENBURG, President of Germany, on Adolf Hitler, 1931, two years before Hitler became Chancellor

If I may judge from my personal knowledge of Herr Hitler, peace and justice are the key-words of his policy.

Conservative MP SIR THOMAS MOORE, October 1933

[My visits to Germany] have given me the impression that there is almost no Great Power with which we are less likely to become involved in war than Germany.

MOORE, in *The Times*, May 1935

Far too many people have an erroneous conception of what the National Socialist regime really stands for. Otherwise they would lay less stress on Nazi dictatorship and much more emphasis on the great social experiment which is being tried out.

SIR NEVILLE HENDERSON, British ambassador to Germany, June 1937

❖

Er . . . If Only They'd Known

Those who imagine that Germany has swung back to its old imperial temper cannot have any understanding of the character of the change. The idea of a Germany intimidating Europe with a threat that its irresistible army might march across frontiers forms no part in the new vision . . . they have no longer the desire themselves to invade any other land.

LLOYD GEORGE, former Prime Minister, writing on his return from visiting Hitler's Germany, *Daily Express*, September 1936

I shall never forget the extraordinarily interesting tour which you organized for me and my friends in Germany last year, during which I had the privilege of meeting the great leader of a great people. I have never doubted the fundamental greatness of Herr Hitler as a man even in moments of profound disagreement with his policy . . . I have never withdrawn one particle of the admiration which I personally felt for him and expressed on my return from Germany.

LLOYD GEORGE, on his meeting with Hitler in September 1936, letter to friend, December 1937

The worst thing Neville Chamberlain ever did was to meet Hitler and let Hitler see him.

LLOYD GEORGE, on the outbreak of war, September 1939

We cannot tell whether Hitler will be the man who will once again let loose upon the world another war . . . or whether he will go down in history as the man who restored honour and peace of mind to the great Germanic nation and brought it back serene, helpful and strong, to the forefront of the European family circle.

WINSTON CHURCHILL, 1935

Germany has been transformed since my last visit several years ago . . . the Reich is the miracle of the twentieth century.

WILLIAM KNUDSEN, president of General Motors, October 1938

Er . . . If Only They'd Known

I do not think there is the slightest prospect of any war. I know . . . how rash it is to prophesy as to the future of international affairs. But nevertheless I do not believe that there is anyone in this room who will contradict me when I say that there has scarcely ever been a period in the world's history when war seemed less likely than it does at present.

VISCOUNT CECIL, the British government representative, opening the League of Nations Assembly session in Geneva, September 1931. A week later Japan invaded Manchuria, the first major challenge for the League. Its failure to settle the dispute started the downward spiral to the Second World War.

Herr Hitler is no longer a problem; his movement has ceased to be a political danger and the whole problem is solved. It is a thing of the past.

GENERAL KURT VON SCHLEICHER, Chancellor of Germany, 15 January 1933. He had become Chancellor six weeks earlier; his government fell a fortnight later when Hitler took over

No danger at all. We've hired him for our act.

FRANZ VON PAPEN, Chancellor of Germany June-December 1932 and new Vice-Chancellor, on Hitler's appointment as Chancellor at the head of a coalition Cabinet limited to containing just two other Nazis, January 1933

It is [Hitler's] set purpose . . . to re-establish Germany on a footing of equality with other nations; and the internal excesses of his regime should not debar foreign statesmanship from examining with an open mind the external claims of the German . . . government.

THE TIMES on the new Hitler government, March 1933

War will not come again . . . [Germany has] a more profound impression than any other of the evil that war causes; Germany's problems cannot be settled by war.

ADOLF HITLER, interview in *Daily Mail*, August 1934

Er . . . If Only They'd Known

I give you my word that there will be no great armaments.

STANLEY BALDWIN, Prime Minister, speech to the International Peace Society, general election campaign, October 1935

The League of Nations will remain . . . the keystone of British foreign policy . . . We shall take no action in isolation, but we shall be prepared to take our part in any collective action decided upon by the League . . .

NATIONAL GOVERNMENT ELECTION MANIFESTO, November 1935 (before the Anglo-Italian agreement in 1937, the four-power Czech settlement in 1938, the 1939 unilateral British guarantee of Poland and the Anglo-French negotiations with Russia in the same year)

Herr Hitler made a statement . . . holding out the olive branch . . . which ought to be taken at face value . . . It is idle to say these statements are insincere.

ARTHUR GREENWOOD, Labour deputy leader, on Hitler's march into the Rhineland and his simultaneous statement that 'Germany has no further territorial claims of any sort in Europe', House of Commons, March 1936

After all, they are only going into their own back garden.

LORD LOTHIAN, on Hitler's remilitarization of the Rhineland, March 1936

There is today a good prospect of restoring those old friendly relations [with Italy] which, until they were recently broken [over the invasion of Abyssinia], had lasted so long that they had become almost traditional between our two countries . . . I only ask you to have a little patience . . . before our agreement with Italy is concluded and published, and then if you are not of my opinion, if you do not believe that it is not the Prime Minister who has been fooled . . . I will be prepared to eat my hat.

NEVILLE CHAMBERLAIN, speaking on appeasement plans with Mussolini's Italy, April 1938

I frankly confess my deep disappointment at an action by the Italian government which has cast a shadow over the genuineness of their intentions to carry out their undertakings.

CHAMBERLAIN, preparing to eat his hat twelve months later, after Mussolini's invasion of Albania, April 1939

Czechoslovakia is not of the remotest concern to us.

Daily Mail article by owner LORD ROTHERMERE, May 1938

Britain never gave any pledge to protect Czechoslovakia . . . No moral obligation rests upon us.

Daily Express statements by *its* owner LORD BEAVERBROOK, 22 September 1938 (on the morning of Chamberlain's second visit to Hitler)

In spite of the hardness and ruthlessness I thought I saw in his face, I got the impression that here was a man who could be relied upon when he had given his word.

NEVILLE CHAMBERLAIN, writing to his sister, after his first meeting with Hitler, Berchtesgaden, September 1938

A quarrel in a far-away country between people of whom we know nothing.

CHAMBERLAIN, characterizing the crisis between Germany and Czechoslovakia over the Sudetenland, September 1938

[Hitler] would not deliberately deceive a man whom he respected and with whom he had been in negotiation.

CHAMBERLAIN reporting to Cabinet, after second meeting with Hitler, Bad Godesberg, September 1938

However much we may sympathize with a small nation confronted by a big and powerful neighbour, we cannot in all circumstances undertake to involve the whole British Empire in a war simply on her account.

CHAMBERLAIN, during Czech crisis, September 1938. A maxim in vogue in the Foreign Office while Chamberlain made his three visits to Hitler during the crisis ran:

If at first you don't concede
Fly, fly, fly again.

Er . . . If Only They'd Known

Peace with honour . . . I believe it is peace for our time.

CHAMBERLAIN, speaking to the crowd in Downing Street, on the Munich Agreement, September 1938

No conqueror returning from a victory on the battlefield has come home adorned with nobler laurels than Mr Chamberlain from Munich yesterday . . . There have been times when such a manifesto [the joint Anglo-German declaration of peace] could be dismissed as a pious platitude . . . The present, it is fair to think, is not such a time.

THE TIMES leader, 'A New Dawn', on the morning after Chamberlain's return from Munich, October 1938

It is my hope, and my belief, that under the new system of guarantees, the new Czechoslovakia will find a greater security than she has ever enjoyed in the past.

NEVILLE CHAMBERLAIN, House of Commons, October 1938

I myself believe that the international guarantee in which we have taken part will more than compensate for the loss of the strategic frontier.

SIR SAMUEL HOARE, Home Secretary, and former Foreign Secretary, defending the Munich settlement, October 1938. Hitler would invade five months later

We never guaranteed the frontiers as they existed. What we did was to guarantee against unprovoked aggression – quite a different thing.

NEVILLE CHAMBERLAIN, House of Commons, November 1938, equivocating after Hitler and Mussolini made border alterations in Czechoslovakia in Hungary's favour without consulting Britain, just a month after Munich

There will be no great war in Europe in 1939.

DAILY EXPRESS, 2 January 1939

Er . . . If Only They'd Known

No man that I know is less tempted than Mr Chamberlain to cherish unreal illusions.

LORD HALIFAX, Foreign Secretary, February 1939

For the Polish Corridor, no British government ever will or ever can risk the bones of a British grenadier.

AUSTEN CHAMBERLAIN, half-brother of Neville, Foreign Secretary, February 1925

In the event of any action which clearly threatened Polish independence and which the Polish government accordingly considered it vital to resist . . . Her Majesty's Government would feel themselves bound at once to lend the Polish government all support in their power. They have given the Polish government an assurance to this effect.

NEVILLE CHAMBERLAIN, announcing the Polish guarantee, House of Commons, March 1939

War today is not only not inevitable, but it is unlikely.

SIR THOMAS INSKIP, Minister for Co-ordination of Defence, August 1939

No enemy bomber can reach the Ruhr. If one reaches the Ruhr, my name is not Goering. You can call me Meyer.

HERMANN GOERING, Nazi air force minister, addressing the Luftwaffe, 1939

The Americans cannot build aeroplanes. They are very good at refrigerators and razor blades.

GOERING, assuring Hitler of the unlikelihood of American air raids on Germany, 1940

I'm an experienced fighter pilot myself. I know what is possible. But I know what isn't too . . . I officially assert that American fighter planes did not reach Aachen . . . I herewith give you an official order that they weren't there.

GOERING, on being told that an Allied fighter had been shot down over German territory, disproving the official view that the Allies did not have a long-range fighter escort capacity, 1943

Er . . . If Only They'd Known

It has been assumed, in my opinion erroneously, that Japan covets these islands [the Philippines]. Just why has never been satisfactorily explained. Proponents of such a theory fail fully to credit the logic of the Japanese mind.

GENERAL DOUGLAS MACARTHUR, 1939. Japan invaded the Philippines three days after Pearl Harbor in 1941

If Japan chose war, the tremendous odds against her would limit the hostilities to a relatively brief period. Should the conflict last six months, a not unreasonably optimistic estimate, the spring of 1942 would see the release the large military and naval forces for action in Europe and the Atlantic.

NEW REPUBLIC, a month before Pearl Harbor, 1941

Whatever happens, the US Navy is not going to be caught napping.

FRANK KNOX, US Secretary of the Navy, 4 December 1941, three days before the Japanese attack on Pearl Harbor

We won't be at war with Japan within forty-eight hours, within forty-eight days, within forty-eight years.

WENDELL WILLKIE, defeated US presidential candidate, at the precise moment his dinner party was interrupted by a telephone call informing him of the attack on Pearl Harbor, December 1941

Japan will be overcome within six months. Her military strength has been sapped by her operations in China. Her economic conditions have been more and more seriously strained . . . Authorities credit her with a good navy but surely the combined fleets of America and Britain should speedily overmatch it.

FORBES MAGAZINE, December 1941, shortly after Pearl Harbor

Defeat of Germany means defeat of Japan, probably without firing a shot.

PRESIDENT ROOSEVELT, supporting the 'Europe first' war strategy, July 1942

Er . . . If Only They'd Known

The British are such clever propagandists, they might well have cooked up the story.

US Congresswoman Jeanette RANKIN, casting the only negative vote against the declaration of war on Japan the day after Pearl Harbor, December 1941

Hitler's missed the bus.

NEVILLE CHAMBERLAIN, House of Commons, 4 April 1940, after the winter of inaction dubbed the 'phoney war' and the 'bore war' which had allowed British forces to build up in France, leading Chamberlain to see a negotiated peace as the most likely outcome. Five days later, Hitler invaded Denmark and Norway; and in May, Holland, Belgium and France

The entry of the United States into the war is of no consequence at all for Germany . . . The United States will not be a threat to us for decades – not in 1945 but at the earliest in 1970 or 1980.

ADOLF HITLER, responding to Soviet Foreign Minister Molotov's concerns about reports of US assistance to Britain, summit meeting, 12 November 1940 (at which time Hitler and Stalin were still technically allies)

We will stay friends with you, whatever happens.

JOSEPH STALIN, to Hans Krebs, acting German military attaché at public diplomatic gathering, Moscow, April 1941. The two dictatorships had signed a non-aggression pact in August 1939. Hitler invaded Russia two months later

Nobody now fears that a Japanese fleet could deal an unexpected blow on our Pacific possessions . . . Radio makes surprise impossible.

JOSEPHUS DANIELS, former US Secretary of the Navy, 1922

Russia is likely to come out of the war the greatest democracy in the world.

CAPT. EDDIE RICKENBACKER, special representative of President Roosevelt, after visit to Russia, 1943

There will no longer be need for spheres of influence, for alliances . . . or any other of the special arrangements through which . . . nations strove to safeguard their security or to promote their interests.

CORDELL HULL, US Secretary of State, on his vision of the post-war world, address to Congress, November 1943

Never in the past has there been any place on the globe where the vital interests of American and Russian people have clashed or even been antagonistic, and there is no reason to suppose there should be now or in the future ever such a place.

DEAN ACHESON, US Under-Secretary of State, 1945

[The Yalta Conference] spells the end of the system of unilateral action, the exclusive alliances, the spheres of influence, the balances of power, and all the other expedients that have been tried for centuries – and have always failed.

PRESIDENT ROOSEVELT, addressing Congress after the Big Three conference with Stalin and Churchill on the post-war settlement, March 1945

[NATO is] a stop-gap and a stop-gap only.

PHILIP NOEL-BAKER, Foreign Office minister, introducing the North Atlantic Treaty Organization treaty to the House of Commons for approval, May 1949. NATO continues

❖

Our defensive perimeter runs from the Aleutians [off Alaska] to Japan, the Ryukyus [Okinawa] and down to the Philippines . . . So far as the military security of other areas in the Pacific is concerned, it must be clear that no person can guarantee these areas against military attack. But it must also be clear that such a guarantee is hardly . . . necessary . . .

DEAN ACHESON, US Secretary of State, speech to the National Press Club, January 1950. His perimeter excluded Korea, and all American forces had just been withdrawn from the peninsula the previous year. The omission is widely believed to have encouraged the North to invade the South, which they did five months later

Er ... If Only They'd Known

Very little. Had they interfered in the first or second months, it would have been decisive. We are no longer fearful of their intervention.

GENERAL DOUGLAS MACARTHUR, commander of allied forces in Korea, September 1950, responding to President Truman's enquiry about the chances of Chinese intervention in the war. Two months later, 850,000 Chinese invaded

It's a pity he knows nothing about economics or social security or finance, but at least we shall be alright with foreign affairs.

JOHN BOYD-CARPENTER, Minister of Transport, 1955, at the time of former Foreign Secretary Anthony Eden's succession of Churchill as Prime Minister. Eden would catastrophically plunge Britain into the Suez crisis the following year, and resign as a consequence after just 21 months in office

[Nasser] is the best sort of Egyptian and a great improvement on the Pashas of the past.

ANTHONY EDEN, then Foreign Secretary, to the Conservative 1922 Committee, after meeting Nasser in Cairo, February 1955

I was asked ... whether our sovereignty was jeopardized and I am saying frankly that it is not.

ALEXANDER DUBCEK, leader of the Prague Spring reforms in Czechoslovakia, press conference, August 1968, days before the Soviet invasion

The major part of the US military task [in Vietnam] can be completed by the end of 1965.

ROBERT MCNAMARA, US Defense Secretary, after visit to South Vietnam, October 1962

Our diplomatic reports indicate that the opposing forces no longer really expect a military victory in South Vietnam.

President LYNDON JOHNSON, 1966

Er . . . If Only They'd Known

Our staying power is what counts in the long and dangerous months ahead. The Communists expect us to lose heart . . . they believe political disagreements in Washington, and confusion and doubt in the United States, will hand them victory in South Vietnam. They are wrong.

JOHNSON, 1967

I seriously doubt if we will have another war. This [Vietnam] is probably the last.

President RICHARD NIXON, 1973

The honeymoon period [is] coming to an end, but it has not ended in divorce or a stand-up fight between husband and wife. The troops have been accepted by both communities and a happy, comfortable married life [is] under way.

DENIS HEALEY, Defence Secretary, visiting Northern Ireland a month after the introduction of British troops to control sectarian troubles, September 1969

Our judgement is that the presence of the Royal Marines garrison . . . is sufficient deterrent against any possible aggression.

MARGARET THATCHER, February 1982, six weeks before the Argentinian invasion of the Falklands

The British won't fight.

LEOPOLDO GALTIERI, President of Argentina, to US Secretary of State Alexander Haig a week after the Argentine invasion of the Falklands, April 1982

The task force involves enormous risks. I say that it will cost this country a far greater humiliation than we have already suffered . . . The attempt will fail.

TONY BENN, April 1982, on plans to recapture the Falklands

Er . . . If Only They'd Known

It is unlikely that Iran could go to war in the next five to ten years with its current inventory without US support on a day-to-day basis.

US SENATE FOREIGN RELATIONS COMMITTEE report, 1977, before the overthrow of the Shah. The Iran-Iraq war broke out in 1980 and lasted until 1988, the longest conventional war of the twentieth century

It'll be over in a few hours.

HAMILTON JORDAN, White House Chief of Staff reacting to the seizure of 63 American Embassy staff in Iran, November 1979. They were held for 444 days

We are in the south to help and protect the Afghan people construct their own democracy. We would be perfectly happy to leave in three years and without firing one shot because our job is to protect the reconstruction.

JOHN REID, Defence Secretary, visiting Helmand province, Afghanistan, April 2006, the location of UK troop deployment, asserting that Britain's mission was fundamentally different to that of the US forces elsewhere in the country (which was 'to go and chase and kill the terrorists who did so much to destroy the twin towers'). Prior to deployment in the anarchic province, just seven British soldiers had been killed in action in the five years since their arrival in Kabul in 2001. In the 12 months from Reid's visit, they had 46 fatalities

Let us demonstrate to the world, as generations of Americans have done before us, that when Americans take on a challenge, they do the job right.

President-elect BILL CLINTON, on the 'invasion' of Somalia by US marines to restore peace in Somalia in Operation Restore Hope, December 1992. Most of the troops were withdrawn by the following May and the task handed over to the United Nations. The rest left in March 1994, and the general view was that the mission had been a failure

We are fully prepared.

GEORGE W. BUSH in video footage recorded the day before Hurricane Katrina struck New Orleans, released in April 2006

Er . . . If Only They'd Known

Katrina exposed serious problems in our response capability at all levels of government. And to the extent that the Federal Government didn't fully do its job right, I take responsibility.

BUSH, September 2005, for the first time holding himself accountable for the government's inadequate response to Hurricane Katrina

Who cares about a little terrorist in Afghanistan?

PAUL WOLFOWITZ, Deputy Defense Secretary, dismissing concerns about Al-Qaeda at an anti-terrorism policy meeting, April 2001

5

Well . . .

On Second Thoughts . . .

We may be surprised, not only by events but by revisions to our own attitudes. Opinions change. The record endures. Those whose job it is to regale the public with pronouncements face, in a long career, an unenviable choice: shall they repeat themselves or contradict themselves? Here are a few who chose the latter . . .

I never should be so presumptuous as to think myself capable of directing the departments of others . . . I do not think our constitution authorizes such a character as that animal called a Prime Minister.

LORD NORTH, Prime Minister, House of Commons, May 1778

[Affairs of state] can hardly be well conducted unless there is a person in the Cabinet capable of leading, of discerning between opinions, of deciding quickly and confidently, and connecting all the operations of government . . .

LORD NORTH to King George III, summer 1778

These wretched colonies . . . are a millstone round our necks.

BENJAMIN DISRAELI, Chancellor of the Exchequer, 1852

In my opinion no minister in this country will do his duty who neglects any opportunity of reconstructing as much as possible our colonial empire, and of responding to those distant sympathies which may become the source of incalculable strength and happiness to this land.

DISRAELI, Opposition leader, 1872

Well . . . On Second Thoughts . . .

One of the greatest of Romans, when asked what were his policies, replied, *Imperium et Libertas* [Empire and Liberty]. That would not make a bad programme for a British ministry.

DISRAELI, Prime Minister, Mansion House speech, 1879

In politics, there is no use looking beyond the next fortnight.

JOSEPH CHAMBERLAIN, President of the Local Government Board under Gladstone and future Colonial Secretary, 1886

It is said that the City is the centre of the world's finance, that the fate of our manufactures therefore is a secondary consideration; . . . Now, I ask you, gentlemen, whether . . . that is not a very short-sighted view.

CHAMBERLAIN, speech to City financiers, London Guildhall, 1904

There is no need to assume the use of force, or, indeed, to talk about it. Such talk is to be strongly deprecated. Not only can it do no good; it is bound to do harm. It must interfere with the progress of diplomacy, and it must increase feelings of insecurity and uncertainty.

NEVILLE CHAMBERLAIN, House of Commons, opposing calls to warn Germany not to use force, beginning of the Sudetenland crisis, March 1938

Our past experience has shown us only too clearly that weakness in armed strength means weakness in diplomacy, and if we want to secure a lasting peace . . . diplomacy cannot be effective unless the consciousness exists . . . that behind the diplomacy is the strength to give effect to it.

CHAMBERLAIN, House of Commons, debate on the Munich Agreement which – temporarily – bought off Hitler at the expense of Czechoslovakia, October 1938

I myself have always deprecated . . . in crisis after crisis, appeals to the Dunkirk spirit as an answer to our problems.

HAROLD WILSON, on Harold Macmillan's use of the patriotic tag during economic difficulties, 1961

Well . . . On Second Thoughts . . .

I believe that the spirit of Dunkirk will once again carry us through to success.

WILSON, now Prime Minister, on his own government's handling of economic difficulties, speech to the party conference, 1964

What the Tories propose [entry into the EEC at the first favourable opportunity] would mean an unacceptable increase in the cost of living . . . an unacceptable increase in our imports bill . . . and a total disruption of our trade with Commonwealth countries.

WILSON, during general election campaign, March 1966

Our purpose is to make a reality of the unity of Western Europe . . . This indeed is something that we have striven for for many years, and I am convinced that if Britain is a member of the united European Community, the chances of our achieving this will be immeasurably greater.

WILSON, Prime Minister, House of Commons, May 1967

I can really see significant long-term opportunities for ordinary people in Britain and in the Six if we could persuade the British public to vote for entry.

TONY BENN, Bristol speech, July 1971

Britain's continuing membership of the Community would mean the end of Britain as a completely self-governing nation.

BENN, letter to constituents, December 1974

I want to put Britain at the very heart of Europe.

JOHN MAJOR, Bonn summit, 1991

We don't want a negative, tentative Britain.

MAJOR, 7 April 1992

I am the biggest Euro-sceptic in the Cabinet.

MAJOR, soon afterwards

The rule of law should be upheld by all political parties. They should neither advise others to break the law, nor encourage others to do so even when they strongly disagree with the legislation put forward by the government of the day.

JAMES CALLAGHAN, Labour shadow employment spokesman, 1972

If the law is a bad law, there is always the contingent right to take action that you would not otherwise take.

CALLAGHAN, retired leader of the Labour Party, 1982

May I remind the House that many of the most progressive and far-reaching educational changes were made by Conservative education ministers . . . among those changes which took place . . . was the movement in Conservative counties towards a new comprehensive system.

MARGARET THATCHER, first speech as Education Secretary, July 1970. In her first three years in office, she received nearly 2,700 proposals for schemes of comprehensive education, and rejected only 115, or less than 4 per cent of them. She approved more comprehensive schools and closed more grammar schools than any other education secretary

The next Conservative government will look forward to discussion and consultation with the trade union movement about the policies that are now needed to save our country.

MARGARET THATCHER, speech to party conference, Brighton, October 1976

The enemy within.

THATCHER'S reported view of trade unions, during miners' strike, 1984–5

We are not in politics to ignore people's worries; we are in politics to deal with them.

MARGARET THATCHER

Many of our troubles are due to the fact that our people turn to politicians for everything.

THATCHER

We must build a society in which each citizen can develop his full potential, both for his own benefit and for the community as a whole.

THATCHER, 1975

We must learn again to be one nation or one day we shall be no nation.

THATCHER, 1978

The mission of this government is much more than the promotion of economic progress. It is to renew the spirit and solidarity of the nation.

THATCHER, July 1979

There is no such thing as Society. There are individual men and women, and there are families.

THATCHER, 1987

Civil servants have not got the expertise at their disposal which a merchant bank has. If they had such expertise, they would probably be working very successfully for a merchant bank.

MARGARET THATCHER, House of Commons, 1967

The sheer professionalism of the British civil service, which allows governments to come and go with a minimum of dislocation and a maximum of efficiency, is something other countries with different systems have every cause to envy.

THATCHER, memoirs, 1993

We secured stable exchange rates in the ERM – and we'll keep our position there.

JOHN MAJOR, election rally, April 1992

The Exchange Rate Mechanism is not an optional extra, an add-on to be jettisoned at the first hint of trouble. It has been and will remain at the heart of our macro-economic policy.

NORMAN LAMONT, Chancellor, July 1992

I was under no illusions when I took Britain into the ERM. I said at the time that membership was no soft option. The soft option, the devaluer's option, the inflationary option, would be a betrayal of our future . . . there is going to be no devaluation, no realignment.

JOHN MAJOR, speech to the Scottish Confederation of British Industry conference, 10 September 1992. Six days later, on 'Black Wednesday', Britain withdrew from the ERM

It is clear that we must not go back into the ERM.

NORMAN LAMONT, addressing the Conservative Party Conference, October 1992

Events made a monkey of us.

JOHN MAJOR, admitting that going into the ERM had been a mistake, March 1997

It is inconceivable that we could transform this society without a major extension of public ownership.

NEIL KINNOCK, *Marxism Today*, 1983

The kind of economy we are faced with is going to be a market economy and we have got to make it work better than the Tories.

KINNOCK, Labour Party conference, 1988

There is nothing in the Labour Party constitution that could or should prevent people from holding opinions which favour Leninist-Trotskyism.

NEIL KINNOCK, then shadow education spokesman, *Broad Left Alliance* journal, October 1982

Maggot extremists.

KINNOCK, Labour leader, describing Militant Tendency activists, February 1986

Well . . . On Second Thoughts . . .

The mild tinkering with the economy proposed by the Social Democrats nowhere near measures up to the problem. A massive reconstruction of industry is needed . . . the resources required to reconstruct manufacturing industry call for enormous state guidance and intervention.

TONY BLAIR, before his election as an MP, 1982

Without an active, interventionist industrial policy . . . Britain faces the future of having to compete on dangerously unequal terms in the EC.

BLAIR, shadow industry spokesman, May 1988

New Labour does not believe it is the job of government to interfere in the running of business.

BLAIR, speech to Nottingham Chamber of Commerce, January 1996

By their disastrous embrace of the Tebbit Bill, they have isolated themselves from organized labour, a fatal mistake for any radical party.

BLAIR on SDP, 1982

The extraordinary proposition [is] advanced that it is the proper role of the government to interfere in the due process of a voluntary organisation . . . It is thoroughly unconscionable and wrong to tell trade unions how to run elections.

BLAIR, back-bencher, opposing the Trade Union Bill requiring unions to hold secret ballots before strike action, House of Commons, November 1983

Having fought long and hard for [their freedoms, unions] will not give them up lightly. We shall oppose the Bill which is a scandalous and undemocratic measure against the trade union movement.

BLAIR, on the same Bill, 1983

The basic elements of that legislation: ballots before strikes, for union elections [and] restrictions on mass picketing are here to stay.

BLAIR, Labour leader, November 1994

Heavens above, that is common sense.

BLAIR, asked whether he would keep the trade union legislation of the 1980s, April 1995

There is no going back on the Thatcherite trade union reforms.

BLAIR, quoted *Daily Telegraph*, January 1996

Parliamentary Labour CND supports the removal of all nuclear weapons from British territory and expresses its solidarity with all campaigners for Peace.

TONY BLAIR, Labour front-bench spokesman, advert signed by him in *Sanity*, May 1986

Labour will retain Britain's nuclear capability, with the number of warheads no greater than the present total.

BLAIR, still before he became party leader, April 1992

The City whizz-kids, with salaries only fractionally less than their greed, now seem not only morally dubious but incompetent.

TONY BLAIR after the share market crash, October 1987

Britain needs successful people in business who can become rich by their success, through the money they earn.

BLAIR, speech to Confederation of British Industry, 1995

Privatized utilities like Telecom and gas and essential industries such as British Airways and Rolls-Royce were sold off by the Tories in the closest thing, post-war, to legalized political corruption . . . in fact it was a unique form of corruption since we were bribed with our own money.

TONY BLAIR, *News on Sunday*, November 1987

The great utilities must be treated as public services and should be owned by the public.

BLAIR, *Enterprise for Labour*, July 1989

Well . . . On Second Thoughts . . .

Let me make it crystal clear that any privatization of the railway system which is there on the arrival of a Labour government will be quickly and effectively returned to public ownership.

JOHN PRESCOTT, Labour front-bench spokesman, September 1993

I am not about to start spraying around commitments as to what we are going to do when the government carries through its proposals.

TONY BLAIR, Labour leader, *Daily Telegraph*, January 1995

I am not going to get into a situation where I am declaring that the Labour government is going to commit sums of money to re-nationalization several years down the line.

BLAIR, January 1995

We are committed to restoring a unified system of railways, with a publicly owned, publicly accountable BR at its core.

BLAIR, Labour conference, 1 October 1996

Instead of wasting hundreds of millions of pounds on compulsory ID cards as the Tory Right demand, let that money provide thousands more police officers on the beat in our local communities.

TONY BLAIR, as Leader of the Opposition, Labour Party conference, October 1995

Through the Identity Cards Bill, we will pave the way for a British identity card – at first voluntary, and then in time, compulsory . . . identity cards, in my judgment, are long overdue.

BLAIR, Prime Minister, House of Commons, November 2004

ID cards are an important part of our manifesto. They are also an important part of trying to protect this country and to deliver a better way for people to protect their identity in the modern world.

BLAIR, Prime Minister, House of Commons, October 2005

The EEC has pushed up prices, especially for food . . . Above all, the EEC takes away Britain's freedom to follow the sort of economic policies we need. These are just two of the reasons for coming out.

BLAIR, campaigning in the Beaconsfield by-election, 1982

We'll negotiate a withdrawal from the EEC which has drained our natural resources and destroyed jobs.

BLAIR, election address, general election 1983

I have always believed that our country can prosper best within Europe.

BLAIR, June 1994

A Labour government will never be cut off or isolated in Europe.

BLAIR, soon after becoming party leader, 1994

I always believed that it was important for Britain to be in Europe. . .

BLAIR, Labour leader, December 1994

I voted for Britain to remain in the EEC in 1975. I fought to persuade my party to become a party of Europe.

BLAIR, speech 30 May 1995

Leaving the European Union . . . would not merely be disastrous for jobs and industry. It would relegate Britain from the premier division of nations with influence and standing.

NEW LABOUR MANIFESTO, July 1996

When Britain's interests are at stake, I am perfectly prepared to be isolated in Europe.

BLAIR, 15 April 1997

Well . . . On Second Thoughts . . .

There is plenty of scope for the House of Commons to fulfil its traditional functions of scrutinizing and amending legislation.

NORMAN LAMONT, defending entry to EEC in House of Commons, 13 July 1973

Our ability to make our own laws without outside interference has gone.

LAMONT, attacking EU, 29 April 1996

Labour is committed to a regional assembly for Wales and to regional assemblies for England.

TONY BLAIR, during Labour leadership contest, June 1994

There is not a consensus about regional assemblies in England . . . We are not committed to regional assemblies in England.

BLAIR, Labour leader, March 1995

At this point, to send a message, particularly abroad, that the whole country or major parts of the country were in quarantine and that democracy had been suspended does not give the image of our country which I believe is accurate.

MICHAEL MEACHER, Secretary of State for the Environment, 20 March 2001, denying the government had any intention of postponing the General Election, which had long been expected in May, because of the outbreak of foot and mouth disease

Postpone until when? One month, two months, six months? In 1967 this disease went on for eight months.

Prime Minister TONY BLAIR, 21 March 2001, denying any intention to postpone the election

We must not send a message that Britain is somehow closed for business.

CHRIS SMITH, Secretary of State for Culture, 31 March 2001

Well . . . On Second Thoughts . . .

This is a decision that has to be taken in the interests of the whole country.

BLAIR, 2 April 2001, announcing a one month delay to local elections, and by implication the General Election, until June 2001

Yes, we are against a single currency.

JOHN PRESCOTT, Labour front-bench spokesman, June 1991

I am not a fan of a single currency, no.

PRESCOTT, July 1994

Would the Prime Minister be in favour of persuading the country that it was right to join a single currency? I say yes to that.

TONY BLAIR, Labour leader, House of Commons, March 1995

The issue of the single currency must be determined by a hard-headed look at its economic practicalities. For Britain, we would need to be convinced that economic conditions would allow it to succeed. We will therefore reserve our options on it.

NEW LABOUR MANIFESTO, July 1996

We'll create two million jobs in five years.

TONY BLAIR, election address, Sedgefield, 1983

I don't actually favour putting a target on it.

BLAIR, Labour leader, on full employment, BBC TV, 12 June 1994

Without ideas, there is no point in being in politics.

JACK STRAW, Labour front-bench spokesman, October 1986

I am a working politician, not a thinker.

STRAW, February 1989

132

Well . . . On Second Thoughts . . .

Markets are poor means of securing welfare and neither the only nor the best way of allocating resources.

Straw, September 1984

We must recognize that a nation of consumers enjoying relatively high living standards becomes literally much more choosy, much more interested in choice and variety. The aspirations of choice are now spreading from consumer goods to public services and rightly so.

Straw, March 1988

We object to the private ownership of capital because of the unacceptable and undemocratic power over other people and over vast resources which it gives to those who hold such concentrations of wealth.

Straw, September 1984

Karl Marx would have supported the policy of Labour's policy review . . . for this process is genuinely dialectical. It is a great pity that Marx's alleged disciples today can't see that.

Straw, July 1988

The basic ideas of socialism − full employment, redistribution of wealth and power, equality, public ownership, collective provision − are as relevant in the 1990s as they were in 1945.

John Prescott, Labour front-bench spokesman, June 1988

I believe in Clause Four − I think there is a role for it.

Prescott, July 1994. Clause Four of the Labour Party constitution was the iconic commitment to a socialist programme of state control and nationalization of industry.

Clause Four was never intended as anything other than something to inspire party activists . . . no Labour government could ever implement anything like Clause Four.

Jack Straw, Labour Party press release, December 1994

Yes, it's the politics of envy. We're envious of their [company directors'] wealth. These people are stinking lousy thieving incompetent scum.

FRANK DOBSON, Labour front-bencher, September 1992

We will ensure that the undeserving rich, the real beneficiaries of the something-for-nothing society, put something back into society.

GORDON BROWN, Labour Party press release, September 1994

Britain needs successful people in business who can become rich by their success, through the money they earn.

TONY BLAIR, Labour leader, speech to Confederation of British Industry, 1995

I would like to confirm that the Labour Party are completely opposed to the privatization of the national air traffic services and under a Labour government they will remain in the public sector.

KEITH BRADLEY, Labour transport spokesman, letter, 5 April 1997

Interviewer: Would you sell off Britain's air traffic control?
Tony Blair: We will certainly look at that. I don't rule it out.

TONY BLAIR, 7 April 1997

It will be strange if there is a landslide.

WILLIAM REES-MOGG, The Times, 1 May, before result declared

Not a surprise, though a somewhat greater avalanche than I expected.

REES-MOGG, The Times, 2 May, after result declared

There are some things we can do on our own. We can abandon the pretence of a British independent deterrent.

DAVID STEEL, Liberal Party leader, 1982

Well . . . On Second Thoughts . . .

We will maintain the deterrent capacity for as long as it is needed.

STEEL, co-leader Liberal/SDP Alliance, general election campaign, 1987

We are fed up with fudging and mudging.

DAVID OWEN, Labour Party conference, shortly before formation of the breakaway SDP, 1980

What is needed is a *socialist* philosophy outside the restrictive confines of much of the present polarized political debate.

OWEN, hardback edition of *Face the Future*, published 1981 (before he led the founding of the breakaway SDP)

What is needed is a *political* philosophy outside the restrictive confines of much of the present polarized political debate.

OWEN, paperback edition of *Face the Future*, published later in 1981 (after the formation of the SDP) (our italics)

I feel a degree of regret that Marshall did not push on and say 'abolish the GLC' because I think it would have been a major saving and would have released massive resources for more productive use.

KEN LIVINGSTONE, 1979, then an Opposition Labour councillor, on the 1977 Marshall Report on the future of the Greater London Council. When later Leader of the GLC, he fought a high profile campaign against abolition legislation in the mid-1980s

I am very glad to support the Energy Conservation Bill. It is long over-due. I shall urge the government to support it.

ROBERT JONES, then a back-bench Conservative MP, 1993

I deplore the Bill . . . Frankly, we have much more practical things to get on with.

JONES, Minister for Energy Conservation, 1994

Well . . . On Second Thoughts . . .

I speak as a champion of the pub trade. [I] want the Chancellor to change his mind. We've had examples … where the impact on a sector has been massive – and the decision has been deferred.

GERRY SUTCLIFFE, junior minister responsible for alcohol licensing, in a statement to a drinks industry trade journal criticising his own government's budget proposals to raise excise duties on alcohol at above inflation rates after public concern over binge drinking, April 2008

My comments do not accurately reflect my views … I fully support the tax measures in the Budget, and the Chancellor's decisions on tax. Alcohol duty increases will go towards helping some of the poorest members of our society.

SUTCLIFFE forced to issue a rapid 'clarifying' statement

The Labour Party is committed to the reintroduction of public ownership of the coal industry.

MARTIN O'NEILL, energy spokesman, House of Commons, March 1994

While we envisage a national role for coal in our energy strategy, we do not intend to re-nationalize the industry.

O'NEILL, speech to the Coal Industry Society conference, November 1994

There has been no change in Labour's policy.

O'NEILL, November 1994

Not only Celtic nationalists feel the need for a significant shift of power away from the centre of British politics . . . One practical answer could be the creation of new regional parliaments. They could strengthen the working of democracy in their areas. With some devolution of powers, they could also take a lot of the workload off Parliament.

KENNETH CLARKE, future Chancellor and opponent of devolution in the 1990s, Birmingham Bow Group pamphlet, 1968

To spend many years in prison for a crime you did not commit is both a terrible thing and one for which release from prison and financial recompense can make amends. Even this injustice cannot be compared to the icy comfort of a posthumous pardon. We cannot but be relieved that the death penalty was not available when we consider the irreparable damage which would have been inflicted on the criminal justice system in this country had innocent people been executed.

MICHAEL HOWARD, Home Secretary, during Commons debate on restoring the death penalty, February 1994. He had previously campaigned for restoration, and voted in its favour in 1990. *'Howard: His league of penal reform is hang 'em'* ran the headline in *Today* when he became Home Secretary in 1993

This is the run-up to the big match which, in my view, should be a walkover.

REAR-ADMIRAL SANDY WOODWARD, commander of the Falklands task force, after the successful capture of South Georgia, 1982

[It] could prove a long and bloody campaign.

WOODWARD, forty-eight hours later

We have stood apart, studiously neutral.

President WOODROW WILSON, speech to Congress, December 1915, about the Great War

America cannot be an ostrich with its head in the sand.

WILSON, speech in Des Moines two months later, February 1916

Government, after all, is a very simple thing.

WARREN HARDING, US President 1921-3, campaign trail

I can't make a damn thing out of this tax problem. I listen to one side and they seem right – and then I talk to the other side and they seem just as right, and here I am where I started. God, what a job!

HARDING, in office

Well . . . On Second Thoughts . . .

Are you certain that you [John F. Kennedy] are quite ready or that the country is quite ready for you in the role of President in 1961? I am greatly concerned and troubled about the situation we are up against in the world now and in the immediate future. That is why I would hope that someone with the greatest possible maturity and experience will be available by this time.

Former President TRUMAN shortly before the Democratic Party convention, July 1960

His [Kennedy's] record . . . is . . . good enough for me.

TRUMAN, campaigning, October 1960

When I make statements, I stick by them.

TRUMAN, campaigning, two days later

The inescapable and harmful by-product of such operations as Social Security . . . has been the weakening of the individual personality and of self-reliance.

US senator BARRY GOLDWATER, 1956

Let me say for perhaps the one millionth time, lest there be any doubt in anyone's mind – that I support the Social Security system and I want to see it strengthened.

GOLDWATER, as Republican candidate, presidential election campaign, 1964

Bob says he offers real leadership – he's right, backwards not forwards.

JACK KEMP, running against George Bush Snr and Bob Dole for the Republican presidential nomination, 1988

The candidate of pain, austerity and sacrifice.

KEMP on Dole, 1988

He has never met a tax he hasn't hiked.

KEMP on Dole, 1988

138

Well . . . On Second Thoughts . . .

When he talks about the future, I'm sure it is time to grab your wallets. I am convinced that Senator Dole has a secret plan to raise taxes on the American people.

KEMP on Dole, 1988

It is the greatest honor of my life to have been asked to run by the greatest American hero.

KEMP, accepting Dole's invitation to be his running mate, presidential campaigns, August 1996

I can't wait to make the case for Bob Dole in every community and every neighbourhood of the United States of America. Our country needs a leader whose stature is equal to that calling, and it's Bob Dole.

KEMP, acceptance speech, August 1996

When he was a quarterback, he played without a helmet.

BOB DOLE'S previous outlook on Kemp

I never want to speak to that man again.

DOLE, after Kemp withdrew from the primary campaign and publicly endorsed rival Steve Forbes, April 1996

I have here in my hand a list of 205 . . . members of the Communist Party and who, nevertheless, are still working and shaping policy in the State Department.

SENATOR JOSEPH MCCARTHY, Senate speech initiating his anti-Communist witchhunt which would transfix America for four years at the height of the Cold War, February 1950. The campaign was characterized by whipped-up paranoia and 'guilt by association' tactics, and little actual proof

[This is] a conspiracy of infamy so black that, when it is finally exposed, its principals shall be for ever deserving of the maledictions of all honest men.

MCCARTHY, speech, Senate, June 1951

I think it is a shoddy, unusual thing to do to use the floor of the Senate to attack your opponent without any proof whatever.

McCARTHY, complaining against attacks on him in the Senate, 1956

It is an unfortunate fact that we can secure peace only by preparing for war.

PRESIDENT JOHN F. KENNEDY, 1960

We will not act prematurely or unnecessarily risk the costs of world-wide nuclear war in which even the fruits of victory would be ashes in our mouth. But neither will we shrink from that risk at any time it must be faced.

KENNEDY, 1962

The basic problems facing the world today are not susceptible to a military solution.

KENNEDY, 1962

I also believe that academic freedom should protect the right of a professor or student to advocate Marxism, Socialism, Communism or any other minority viewpoint – no matter how distasteful to the majority.

RICHARD NIXON

What are our schools for if not indoctrination against Communism?

NIXON

A government makes no more fateful decision than the decision to go to war. The President should want to share that decision with Congress.

WARREN CHRISTOPHER, US Secretary of State, on the President's right to decide whether to send US troops into battle, 1982

Well . . . On Second Thoughts . . .

We can't tie the hands of the President.

CHRISTOPHER, responding to Congress's wish to be involved in decisions on sending troops to Bosnia, September 1994

Thank you for contacting me to express your opposition . . . to the early use of military force by the US against Iraq. I share your concerns. On January 11, I voted in favour of a resolution that would have insisted that economic sanctions be given more time to work and against a resolution giving the President the immediate authority to go to war.

JOHN KERRY, then Massachusetts senator, letter to a constituent 22 January 1991 on the first Gulf War

Thank you for contacting me to express your support for the actions of President Bush in response to the Iraqi invasion of Kuwait. From the outset of the invasion, I have strongly and unequivocally supported President Bush's response to the crisis and the policy goals he has established with our military deployment in the Persian Gulf.

KERRY, letter to the same constituent, 31 January 1991

The most important thing is for us to find Osama bin Laden. It is our number one priority and we will not rest until we find him.

GEORGE W. BUSH, 13 September 2001

I want justice . . . There's an old poster out West, as I recall, that said, 'Wanted: Dead or Alive'.

BUSH, 17 September 2001

I don't know where Bin Laden is. I have no idea and really don't care. It's not that important. It's not our priority.

BUSH, March 2002

I am truly not that concerned about him.

BUSH, responding to a question about bin Laden's whereabouts, March 2002

Well . . . On Second Thoughts . . .

One of the interesting things people ask me, now that we're asking questions, is, can you ever win the war on terror? Of course you can.

BUSH, April 2004

I don't think you can win [the war on terror].

BUSH, 30 August 2004

Make no mistake about it, we are winning and we will win [the war on terror].

BUSH, 31 August 2004

I'm worried about an opponent who uses nation building and the military in the same sentence.

GEORGE W. BUSH, on Al Gore, Presidential election campaign, November 2000

If we don't stop extending our troops all around the world in nation-building missions, then we're going to have a serious problem coming down the road.

BUSH, Presidential candidate, opposing taking on nation-building around the world, October 2000

I don't think our troops ought to be used for what's called nation building. I think our troops ought to be used to fight and win war. I think our troops ought to be used to help overthrow a dictator when it's in our best interests. But in [Somalia], it was a nation-building exercise. And same with Haiti. I wouldn't have supported either.

BUSH, Presidential election campaign, October 2000

We will be changing the regime of Iraq, for the good of the Iraqi people.

BUSH supporting nation-building in Iraq, March 2003

Well . . . On Second Thoughts . . .

So, creating a Cabinet office doesn't solve the problem. You still will have agencies within the federal government that have to be coordinated. So the answer is that creating a Cabinet post doesn't solve anything.

ARI FLEISCHER, White House spokesman, on Bush's opposition to creating a Homeland Security Department, March 2002

So tonight, I ask the Congress to join me in creating a single, permanent department with an overriding and urgent mission: securing the homeland of America and protecting the American people.

GEORGE W. BUSH announcing the Department in an address to the nation, June 2002

We developed a bold approach under which, if the North addressed our long-standing concerns, the United States was prepared to take important steps that would have significantly improved the lives of the North Korean people. Now that North Korea's covert nuclear weapons program has come to light, we are unable to pursue this approach.

BUSH, halting the programme to offer North Korea incentives to stop developing nuclear capacity, November 2002

Well, we will work to take steps to ease their political and economic isolation. So there would be – what you would see would be some provisional or temporary proposals that would only lead to lasting benefit after North Korea dismantles its nuclear programs. So there would be some provisional or temporary efforts of that nature.

SCOTT MCCLELLAN, White House spokesman announcing Bush's approach to incentivize North Korea, June 2004

I don't think you give timelines to dictators.

BUSH, on dealing with the illicit nuclear weapons programmes of the Iranian and North Korean regimes, September 2004

Well . . . On Second Thoughts . . .

I am pleased with the agreements reached today . . . These talks represent the best opportunity to use diplomacy to address North Korea's nuclear programs.

BUSH, 13 February 2007, changing tack again commending the six-party agreement in Beijing that gave a 60-day deadline for North Korea to close down its experimental nuclear complex

I know how disheartened Palestinians are by the decisions to build the barrier . . . We do not need another barrier to peace. Provocative and counterproductive measures only harm Israelis.

Senator JOHN KERRY on Israel's project to build a wall to separate Israeli and Palestinian populations, October 2003

A legitimate act of self-defence.

KERRY, describing the wall, February 2004

6

Ahem . . .

I May Have Misled You

Intentions change. Though consistency of purpose is thought a virtue in public life, those who lead often find that the first draft of their plans later requires a little tweak here and there. Sometimes, they were lying first time; sometimes they really meant it . . .

Read my lips. No new taxes.

GEORGE BUSH SNR, presidential campaign, 1988. (He won – then raised them a year later, with the second biggest tax rise in American history)

We don't need quick political promises out in a parking lot somewhere, to be forgotten when the election's over.

BUSH, campaign 1988

We raised taxes on the American people and we put this country right into a recession.

DAN QUAYLE, apologizing for President Bush's 'no new taxes' pledge, September 1992

The President is not a statistician.

SCOTT McCLELLAN, White House press secretary, February 2004, after the second Bush Administration backed away from an earlier forecast that the US economy would gain 2.6 million jobs in the year

Ahem . . . I May Have Misled You

There are some in this country who fear that in going into Europe we shall in some way sacrifice independence and sovereignty. These fears, I need hardly say, are completely unjustified.

EDWARD HEATH, Prime Ministerial television broadcast to mark Britain joining the European Community, January 1973. Contrary to this reassuring assertion, a confidential Foreign Office paper, produced in 1971, had warned the government that membership would entail very substantial constraints on Britain's powers of self-government. It only became known to the public when released in 2001 under the 30-year rule

The government have no plans to extend the scope of VAT to any items which are currently zero-rated and have no need to do so.

JOHN MAJOR, House of Commons, 9 March 1992

We have no plans to widen the scope of VAT.

MAJOR, general election press conference, March 1992

I propose over the next two years to end the zero rate of VAT on fuel and power . . . VAT will be charged at 8 per cent from 1 April 1994 and 17.5 per cent from 1 April 1995.

NORMAN LAMONT, Chancellor of the Exchequer, Budget statement, March 1993, announcing the imposition of VAT on domestic gas, electricity and coal

We want no wars of conquest. We must avoid the temptation of territorial aggression.

WILLIAM MCKINLEY, American President, inaugural address, March 1897. Within three years, he oversaw the largest accumulation of overseas territory in American history, annexing Hawaii, Cuba, Puerto Rico, Guam, Samoa and the Philippines, turning the United States into an imperial power

Forceful intervention in Chechnya is unacceptable. If we violate this principle, the Caucasus will rise up. There will be so much terror and blood that afterwards no one will forgive us.

BORIS YELTSIN, Russian President, August 1994. Four months later, he ordered Russian troops into Chechnya. To date, an estimated 30,000 civilians have died in the war

Ahem . . . I May Have Misled You

The military phase of the Chechen campaign is effectively over.

YELTSIN, after Russian troops captured the Chechen parliament building, January 1995. A vicious guerrilla war ensued

I fight on. I fight to win.

MARGARET THATCHER, after failing to win the required majority in the first round of the Conservative Party leadership contest, 21 November 1990

I have concluded that the unity of the party and the prospects of victory in a general election would be better served if I stood down.

THATCHER, withdrawing from the leadership contest, 22 November 1990

This is not a lightly given pledge. It is a promise. We shall achieve the 500,000 target, and we shall not allow any developments, any circumstances, however adverse, to deflect us from our aim.

HAROLD WILSON, Prime Minister, on Labour's programme of council house building, general election campaign, March 1966. The government was to fall short of that figure by 100,000

There are too many uncertainties for it to be possible for anyone to say exactly how many will be built.

ANTHONY GREENWOOD, Wilson's Minister of Housing, abandoning the government's target, January 1968

There was no impropriety whatsoever in my acquaintanceship with Miss Keeler . . . I shall not hesitate to issue writs for libel and slander if scandalous allegations are made or repeated outside the House.

JOHN PROFUMO, Secretary of State for War, statement in the House of Commons, March 1963

Ahem . . . I May Have Misled You

In my statement I said that there had been no impropriety in this association. To my very deep regret I have to admit that this is not true, and that I misled you and my colleagues, and the House.

PROFUMO, resignation letter to Prime Minister Harold Macmillan, June 1963. (It prompted the doggerel:
'What have you done?' cried Christine,
'You've wrecked the whole party machine.
To lie in the nude may be rude,
But to lie in the House is obscene.')

[There is] no question that an admission of making false statements to government officials and interfering with the FBI and the CIA is an impeachable offence.

BILL CLINTON on Richard Nixon during the Watergate scandal, 1974

I ask that all Americans demonstrate in their personal and public lives . . . the high ethical standards that are essential to good character and to the continued success of our Nation.

CLINTON during National Character Counts Week, 1997

I want you to listen to me. I'm going to say this again. I did not have sexual relations with that woman, Miss Lewinsky. I never told anybody to lie, not a single time – never. These allegations are false.

CLINTON, notoriously misleading America, 26 January 1998

I honor her.

CLINTON, referring to his wife, Hillary, State of the Union Address, 27 January 1998

When I was alone with Ms Lewinsky on certain occasions . . . I engaged in conduct that was wrong. These encounters did not consist of sexual intercourse. They did not constitute sexual relations as I understood that term to be defined at my January 17th, 1998 deposition. But they did involve inappropriate intimate contact.

CLINTON's explanation, Grand Jury testimony, 17 August 1998

Ahem . . . I May Have Misled You

I did have a relationship with Ms Lewinsky that was not appropriate. In fact, it was wrong. It constituted a critical lapse in judgment and a personal failure on my part for which I am solely and completely responsible.

CLINTON, national broadcast, after giving evidence to the Grand Jury, 17 August 1998

It depends on what the meaning of the word 'is' is.

CLINTON'S Grand Jury Testimony, August 1998. He elaborated, 'If "is" means "is and never has been" that's one thing – if it means "there is none", that was a completely true statement'. He also contended that 'sexual relations' did not to him mean 'sexual intercourse', which he denied having with the former White House intern

If [Mr Clinton] is the person who has oral sex performed on them then the contact is not with anything . . . but with the lips of another person.

CLINTON explaining, through his lawyer, why he thought oral sex had not fallen into the definition of sexual relations

Our society should be purged of the perverts who provide the media with pornographic material while pretending it has some redeeming social value under the public's 'right to know'.

KENNETH STARR, US lawyer, speaking in 1987

The report contained pages of pornographic detail and damning commentary . . . Don't blame the messenger because the message is unpleasant.

STARR, a decade later, when special prosecutor of the Clinton–Monica Lewinsky sex scandal. His 453-page report in September 1998 was widely criticised in the US Congress and media for its inclusion of graphic details of the pair's encounters

My colleagues and I will never use words to support actions which exploit or intensify divisions in our society.

EDWARD HEATH, on becoming Prime Minister, June 1970. In October he published plans for reform of the trade unions, culminating in the 1971 Industrial Relations Act, which was bitterly opposed by the unions. In July he had opened negotiations for Britain's entry into the EEC, which polarized most of the rest of the country

A social democratic party without deep roots in the working class movement would quickly fade into an unrepresentative intellectual sect.

Roy Jenkins, 1972

The Labour Party is and always has been an instinctive part of my life.

Jenkins, 1973

There is a lot of talk about a centre party – and that I might lead it. I find this idea profoundly unattractive.

Jenkins, 1973

If I got fed up with the Labour Party, I should leave politics altogether.

Shirley Williams, 1979

We believe that a centre party would have no roots, no principles, no philosophy, and no values.

Williams, 1980

I would not join a centre party because I feel the whole idea is wrong.

Williams, 1980

There is no way I could have been anything but a socialist. It would have been a clear revolt against my whole upbringing and family background.

Williams, 1980

We are the heart of the party. We are what the Labour movement is all about. We are going to win and we are going to keep it that way.

William Rodgers, on being a Labour moderate, 1977. In 1981 he was one of the 'Gang of Four' founders of the SDP. So were Williams and Jenkins

There is one big obstacle in the way of all our plans for change. It is the greatest legacy of the Tory years – disillusion with politics itself. And if we want to remove it we must show that our politics is not theirs. Not just that our vision for Britain is different, but also our means of achieving it. A new politics – a politics of courage, honesty and trust.

TONY BLAIR, as Leader of the Opposition, Labour Party conference, October 1994

I suspect Blair and his government are going to be as strongly identified with the loss of public trust as Major's was with sleaze. The public certainly feel let down over the period.

SIR ALISTAIR GRAHAM, chairman of the Committee on Standards in Public Life, the sleaze watchdog created after the 1994 parliamentary 'cash for questions' scandal, March 2007. Graham listed seven major lapses – the 'cash for honours' scandal; how arguments were presented in the lead up to the Iraq war; blocking a corruption investigation into a British arms' supplier and Saudi Arabia; appointing an independent figure to investigate improper behaviour by Ministers and failing to refer a single case to them; ignoring evidence of risks in postal voting, undermining public faith in the electoral system; undue reliance on 'spin' to recycle announcements; politicising the civil service

Only tabloid journalists now stand between ministers and the bottom of the league.

GRAHAM, same interview

We will be open with the people about tax.

TONY BLAIR, BBC radio interview, November 1996, before becoming Prime Minister

There are no concealed tax increases . . . There is no evasion, no double-dealing, no hidden agenda.

BLAIR, press conference, January 1997. In the 10 years of his premiership, his Chancellor Gordon Brown became renowned for using indirect and obscure 'stealth' taxes – in 2007 the Conservative Opposition alleged there had been 101 of them – rather than more noticeable ways to increase the Government's tax take

Ahem . . . I May Have Misled You

I want to protect state pensions

Tony Blair, writing in the *Daily Mirror*, June 1994

The unemployed youngster has no right to steal your radio. But let's get just as serious about catching the people in the City with an eye on your pension.

Blair, Labour Party conference, October 1994. Revelations in April 2007, towards the end of his premiership, showed his Chancellor's abolition of tax concessions for pension schemes shortly after coming to office in 1997 ended up devastating Britain's pension system over the following decade. The industry estimated the move had cost pension schemes £100 billion

The average length of time in office for ministers of education since the First World War is less than two years . . . It has got to change. Under Labour, it will. I want my ministers to expect to take responsibility for seeing a strategy through . . .

Tony Blair, speech December 1996. In his ten years of office, Blair went through five Secretaries of State for Education – David Blunkett, Estelle Morris, Charles Clarke, Ruth Kelly and Alan Johnson. The fifth was appointed in May 2006, just nine years after Labour took office, giving an average for each minister of . . . less than two years

I do believe that there would be less crime under Labour – I believe that absolutely sincerely.

Tony Blair, BBC television interview, October 1994

There must be a comprehensive attack on crime and its causes instead of a search for easy headlines.

Blair, writing in *The Times*, November 1996

A thug might think twice about kicking your gate, throwing traffic cones around your street, or hurling abuse into the night sky if he thought he might get picked up by the police, taken to a cashpoint and asked to pay an on-the-spot fine of, for example, £100

Blair, proposing instant fines for street hooligans, June 2000

Ahem . . . I May Have Misled You

I think that the whole process of thinking that people who are raging drunk, or indeed those who are being disorderly or even violent, can be made quiescent to go to a cashpoint, will cause us some difficulties.

SIR JOHN EVANS, president of the Association of Chief Police Officers, reacting to the Prime Minister's plan

One or two chief constables said it was not a goer.

CHARLES CLARKE, then the Home Office minister in charge of youth justice, two days after Blair's speech acknowledging there was a problem with the concept. He maintained that the Prime Minister was 'using a metaphor' when he spoke about frogmarching hooligans to cashpoints

[An on-the-spot fine] was not seen by officers as the best way of proceeding.

CLARKE, a week later announcing the abandonment of the plan

We won't [scrap Conservative immigration laws]. Under this Government, thousands of people every year settled in Britain illegally. We are determined to clamp down on this.

TONY BLAIR, writing in the *Sun*, March 1997. In the next ten years, asylum seeking and illegal immigration into Britain ballooned. In 2006, he came under fire for admitting that the government still did not have official estimates for the scale of illegal immigration. That May, Tony McNulty, the Immigration Minister, estimated that between 310,000 and 570,000 was 'roughly in the ball park' of how many illegal immigrants were in the country. He added it would take a decade to remove them

If there are further steps to European integration, the people should have their say at a general election or in a referendum.

TONY BLAIR, newly-elected Prime Minister, 1997, on plans for a European Constitution

I see no case for having a referendum on the new EU Constitution. We don't govern this country by referendum.

BLAIR, May 2003, as the Constitution became more of a reality

Ahem . . . I May Have Misled You

It's essentially the same proposal as the old Constitution.

MARGOT WALLSTROM, EU Commissioner for Institutional Relations and
Communications, on the contrast between the Lisbon Treaty and the
'abandoned' EU Constitution, Svenska Dagbladet, June 2007

I have taken on the work of comparing the draft of the new Treaty
of Lisbon with the Constitution on the 'nine essential points'
published on this blog. To my surprise and, to tell the truth, to my
great satisfaction, these nine points reappear word for word in the
new project. Not a comma has changed! The only thing is that you
have to really look for them because they are dispersed in the
texts the new Treaty refers to, namely the Treaties of Rome and
Maastricht.

VALERY GISCARD D'ESTAING, former French president and chief architect of the
EU Constitution, on his blog, November 2007

Taken as a whole, the [Lisbon] Reform Treaty produces a general
framework which is substantially equivalent to the Constitutional
Treaty…

House of Commons EUROPEAN SCRUTINY COMMITTEE report, 9 October 2007

When it was a constitutional treaty, nine Governments in Europe
said there should be a referendum. As it is no longer a
constitutional treaty, only one Government – the Irish, who are
legally obliged to do so – are having a referendum. This has been
through constitutional courts in Denmark and Holland, which
agreed that this is not a constitutional treaty. In fact, the first words
of the Brussels declaration are that the constitutional concept has
been abandoned.

Prime Minister GORDON BROWN, House of Commons, 17 March 2008,
defending the government's decision not to hold a referendum on the Lisbon
Treaty. In its election manifesto in 2005, the party had promised one on the
planned EU Constitution

If this were a constitutional treaty, we would hold a referendum.
… But the constitutional concept was abandoned, and that is why
the nine countries that proposed a referendum … are not holding
one.

BROWN, House of Commons, 5 March 2008

Ahem . . . I May Have Misled You

The Taoiseach and I have had a meeting this morning. We have discussed the European constitution and how that can move forward over the next few months.

BROWN, freudian slip opening a press conference after meeting his Irish counterpart Bertie Ahern during his first visit to Northern Ireland as Prime Minister, July 2007, according to the transcript published on the Prime Minister's official website

Not for the first time, European eyes are on Ireland this year because of the Treaty referendum. I am not going there to tell Irish people how to vote. My interest is that there be a proper debate and discussion of all the issues. In that regard I think the Irish National Forum is an example to many other countries. … To me, this is the essence of grassroots democracy.

MARGOT WALLSTROM, EU Commissioner for Institutional Relations and Communications, official blog, 27 February 2008

Inefficient decision making.

WALLSTROM'S reported comments according to the *Sunday Times*, June 2008, a few hours after the Irish referendum rejected the Lisbon Treaty

I lied. I lied. My credibility will be in shreds. I lied. If this gets out, I'll be destroyed.

Chancellor GORDON BROWN'S alleged remarks, first published in September 2000, on Formula One motor racing chief Bernie Ecclestone's secret £1 million donation to New Labour four months before its 1997 election victory. Scandal erupted when the government announced the following November motor racing's exemption from a tobacco advertising ban

I do not lie – I wouldn't lie.

BROWN, responding to the charges of a cover-up, September 2000

Our acts must be guided by one single, hard-headed thought: keeping America out of this war.

US President FRANKLIN D. ROOSEVELT, September 1939

We are keeping out of the wars that are going on in Europe and Asia.

ROOSEVELT, April 1940

Ahem . . . I May Have Misled You

We will not send our men to take part in European wars.

ROOSEVELT, July 1940

And while I am talking to you mothers and fathers, I give you one more assurance. I have said this before, but I shall say it again and again and again: Your boys are not going to be sent into any foreign wars.

ROOSEVELT, October 1940

The [Cuban] movement is not a Communist movement. . . We have no intention of expropriating US property.

FIDEL CASTRO, visiting Washington 'as a good neighbour' shortly after taking power in 1959, declaring his wish to allay fears about his new regime. By 1961 the new government had expropriated over $1 billion of US property

I am a Marxist-Leninist and will be one until the day I die.

CASTRO, December 1961

We have to be ready to conduct the necessary reforms to adapt our country and our economy to the present world situation.

CASTRO, January 1995

I believe that all of us ought to retire relatively young.

FIDEL CASTRO, Cuban leader, interview January 1967, on the eighth anniversary of his revolution. He eventually called it a day more than forty years later in February 2008, at the age of 81

We shall never stop until we can go back home and Israel is destroyed. The goal of our struggle is the end of Israel and there can be no compromises or mediations.

YASSER ARAFAT, Palestinian leader, 1970

Mr Prime Minister . . . the PLO recognizes the right of Israel to exist in peace and security [and] renounces the use of terrorism and other acts of violence.

ARAFAT, signing the Middle East peace deal with Israel at the White House, September 1993

Ahem . . . I May Have Misled You

We intend to make to the alliances of which we are members a contribution related to our economic capability while recognizing that our security lies fundamentally in Europe and must be based on the North Atlantic alliance.

WILSON, statement to the House of Commons, January 1968 announcing the withdrawal of a military presence East of Suez from 1971

The essential feature of our current defence policy is a readiness to recognize that political and economic realities reinforce the defence arguments for concentrating Britain's military role in Europe.

WILSON's Defence White Paper, February 1969

There will not be, under any conditions, any intervention in Cuba by the United States armed forces. This government will do everything it possibly can . . . to make sure that there are no Americans involved in any actions inside Cuba.

President JOHN F. KENNEDY, news conference, 12 April 1961. He kept America's word, technically – the CIA-inspired Bay of Pigs operation that followed four days later used predominantly Cuban exiles. They were, however, equipped with US military kit including eight B-26 bombers painted by the CIA to resemble Cuban air force planes. The involvement of some US military was revealed when four American B-26 pilots were shot down in the bombing raids

Should I become President I will not risk American lives by permitting any other nation to drag us into the wrong war at the wrong place at the wrong time through an unwise commitment that is unwise militarily, unnecessary to our security, and unsupported by our allies.

KENNEDY, presidential campaign, October 1960. At the time, America's involvement in Vietnam consisted of 700 military advisers

If necessary I would consider the use of US forces to help South Vietnam resist Communist pressures.

KENNEDY, now President, press conference, May 1961. By early 1962, there were 4,000 military 'advisers'; by the end of the year, 12,000. When Kennedy was assassinated, there were 16,000 committed

Ahem . . . I May Have Misled You

We Americans know . . . the risks of spreading conflict. We still seek no wider war.

President LYNDON JOHNSON, August 1964

We are not about to send American boys nine or ten thousand miles away from home to do what Asian boys ought to be doing for themselves.

JOHNSON, election speech, October 1964. The first US ground troops went into Vietnam the following March. By the end of 1965 there were 185,000, reaching at their peak (1969) over half a million

There is and will be, as long as I am President, peace for all Americans.

JOHNSON, October 1964

Let every nation know . . . we shall pay any price, bear any burden, meet any hardship, support any friend, oppose any foe to assure the survival and the success of liberty.

President JOHN F. KENNEDY, inaugural address, 1961

America cannot – and will not – conceive all the plans, design all the programmes, execute all the decisions and undertake all the defence of the free nations of the world.

RICHARD NIXON, presidential address to Congress, February 1970. He was to end the war

The Germans, if this government is returned, are going to pay every penny; they are going to be squeezed, as a lemon is squeezed – until the pips squeak.

SIR ERIC GEDDES, First Lord of the Admiralty, general election campaign, December 1918, immediately after the First World War. Germany eventually paid one-eighth of the sum originally demanded

I would flatly oppose any grant by the federal government to all states in the Union for educational purposes.

DWIGHT EISENHOWER, 1949

The federal government should serve as an effective agent in dealing with this [classroom shortage] problem.

EISENHOWER, now President, State of the Union address, 1955

The federal government contributes to economic growth when it takes its part . . . in providing public facilities such as . . . educational institutions.

EISENHOWER, 1955

I don't believe myself it is necessary for the people as a whole to have their living standards lowered in order to conquer inflation.

DENIS HEALEY, Chancellor of the Exchequer, election campaign, September 1974

If we tighten our belt now we can start moving ahead next year and we'll be in far better shape then than at any time since the war.

HEALEY, Budget broadcast, April 1975

I do not think that this would be the right moment to cut people's standard of life in terms of private consumption any further.

JAMES CALLAGHAN, Prime Minister, House of Commons, July 1976

Let me say that of course there has been a fall in people's standard of life. And it has fallen this year and will fall again next year.

CALLAGHAN, BBC TV, October 1976

The standard of living has been deliberately reduced by the government over the last eighteen months in order that we should get ourselves financially straight again. That should be a matter for congratulation and not for recrimination.

DENIS HEALEY, March 1977

NO . . . Australia is NOT going into recession.

PAUL KEATING, Australian Treasurer, November 1989

Ahem . . . I May Have Misled You

This is the recession that Australia had to have.

KEATING, January 1990

The Labour Party gives defence of the pound the first priority. We shall need to sacrifice all other considerations to make sterling strong.

HAROLD WILSON, shadow Chancellor, February 1958

Devaluation would be regarded all over the world as an acknowledgement of defeat, a recognition that we are not on a springboard but a slide.

WILSON, July 1961

Devaluation, whether of sterling, or of the dollar, or both, would be a lunatic, self-destroying operation.

WILSON, Opposition leader, 1963

The facilities for further borrowing which have been . . . built up these past few years have given us a firm base from which we can advance without panic measures, without devaluation, without stop-and-go measures.

WILSON, October 1964. Over the next six years Britain had them all

From now the pound abroad is worth 14 per cent or so less in terms of other currencies. It does not mean, of course, that the pound here in Britain, in your pocket or purse, or in your bank has been devalued.

WILSON, television statement announcing devaluation, 1967

Let me say this very slowly indeed. In fact, if you can, watch my lips. No selection either by examination or interview under a Labour Government.

DAVID BLUNKETT, shadow education minister, Labour party conference, 1995

I'm not hunting grammar schools . . . Watch my lips was a joke.

DAVID BLUNKETT, when Secretary of State for Education, March 2000, after parents in Yorkshire had voted to retain selection in ballots allowed for under 1998 education legislation introduced by Blunkett

Ahem . . . I May Have Misled You

I will say then that I am not, nor ever have been in favour of bringing about in any way the social and political equality of the white and black races . . . There is a physical difference between the white and black races which I believe will for ever forbid the two races living together on terms of social and political equality. And inasmuch as they cannot so live, while they do remain together there must be the position of superior and inferior, and I as much as any other man am in favour of having the superior position assigned to the white race.

ABRAHAM LINCOLN, campaigning for the Senate, August 1858

Even when you cease to be slaves, you are yet far removed from being placed on an equality with the white race. You are cut off from many of the advantages which the other race enjoys. It is better for us both to be separated.

LINCOLN, then President, during a meeting with free Negro leaders, White House, August 1862

If my name ever goes into history, it will be for this act, and my whole soul is in it.

LINCOLN, signing the Emancipation Proclamation, ending slavery in the United States, January 1863

The central act of my administration, and the great event of the nineteenth century . . . It is a momentous thing to be the instrument . . . of the liberation of a race.

LINCOLN, describing the Emancipation Proclamation, 1863

We've got a big job to do in some of those inner cites, a really big job. Our policies are geared – education and housing – to help people in the inner cities . . .

MARGARET THATCHER, victory speech inside No 10, election night, June 1987

It would be quite wrong to indicate that there is a pot of gold and all you have to do is say 'Please, I want more [for the inner cities].'

THATCHER, September 1987

Ahem . . . I May Have Misled You

We must always be willing to help the vulnerable and disadvantaged . . . Christianity is full of mercy and compassion.

TONY BLAIR, 7 April 1996

Interviewer: Do you give money to beggars?
Tony Blair: I don't, no.

BLAIR, interview in *The Big Issue* magazine, January 1997

It is right to be intolerant of people homeless on the street.

BLAIR, January 1997

If you're British and can give an address, free money is available from social security . . . Never be reticent about claiming [benefits]. For whatever reason the so-called welfare state was brought into being, it can and must be used to its full extent.

Advice to students in a handbook edited by 22-year-old GORDON BROWN, future Chancellor, while a student at Edinburgh University in the 1970s, revealed in April 2007 shortly before he became Prime Minister. The booklet gave further advice on conning free food from hotels and declared there was nothing wrong being a 'parasite'

I do not think that politicians should get into the position of trying to moralise. I, as the son of a Church of Scotland minister, I'm not going to moralise about people's circumstances I don't know about.

New Prime Minister, GORDON BROWN, July 2007, seizing the moral high ground by criticising the Tories for 'moralising'

In September, we will have a report that will look at ... the incidence and prevalence of [gambling] and its social effects. I hope that ... we can look at whether regeneration in the areas for the super-casinos may be a better way of meeting their economic and social needs than the creation of super-casinos.

GORDON BROWN, moralising and abandoning one of his predecessor's keynote policies just two weeks after becoming Prime Minister, House of Commons, 11 July 2007

[W]e will strengthen the police. Yes we will strengthen our laws. But preventing crime for me also means all of us as a community setting boundaries between what is acceptable and unacceptable behaviour – with clear penalties for stepping over the line. Boundaries that reflect the words I was taught when I was young – words upon which we all know strong communities are founded: discipline, respect, responsibility.

BROWN, two months later in his first speech to the Labour Party conference as Prime Minister, September 2007

For tackling climate change – the world's biggest market failure – [is] not just an environmental and economic imperative, but a moral one.

BROWN, as Chancellor, launching the Stern Review on the economics of climate change, October 2006

Healthcare is not a privilege to be purchased but a moral right secured for all.

BROWN speech on the National Health Service, January 2008

Hunger is a moral challenge to each one of us as global citizens.

BROWN, article headlined 'PM – Food crisis a "moral challenge for everyone"', written for Downing Street website on the world food crisis, April 2008

The Prime Ministers noted that climate change represented the greatest moral and economic challenge globally for the future.

Communiqué issued after BROWN met his new Australian counterpart, KEVIN RUDD, April 2008

A global society where people anywhere and everywhere can discover their shared values . . . and . . . join together with people in other countries in a single moral universe to bring about change.

BROWN, setting out his vision, speech to the Church of Scotland General Assembly, May 2008

Ahem . . . I May Have Misled You

And when conscience is joined to conscience, moral force to moral force . . . think how much our power to do good and our power to change lives can achieve.

BROWN, launching an alliance of 20 global business leaders to help meet global development tagets, May 2008

[A]n inherently moral endeavour that can save and improve the lives of thousands and, over time, millions of people.

BROWN, writing in the *Observer*, May 2008, at the height of public controversy over his government's proposals to reform embryology legislation to allow stem cell research

I want Britain to be far more upwardly mobile as a country. At its core I think this is a great moral endeavour . . .

BROWN, launching a campaign to improve Britain's 'social mobility', June 2008

I don't think that anyone actually wants that to be a priority of the Labour Party at the moment . . . I don't think anyone is saying now . . . that this is the sort of thing we should focus on.

TONY BLAIR, asked whether he opposed the dropping of Labour's historic Clause Four on nationalization, during the party leadership campaign, June 1994. After becoming leader the following month, he announced the review of Clause Four at the party conference in September, leading a successful high-profile campaign in 1995 for its scrapping

Yes, I support repeal of the ban on gays and lesbians serving in the United States armed forces.

BILL CLINTON, presidential campaign, 1992

I intend to keep my commitment.

CLINTON, five days after his inauguration as President, January 1993

I do not propose any changes in the code of military conduct. None. Zero. I do not believe that anything should be done in terms of behaviour that would undermine unit cohesion or morale.

CLINTON, May 1993

Ahem . . . I May Have Misled You

I do not think we should ever pick a fight with the President of the United States if it's avoidable.

NEWT GINGRICH, Speaker of the US House of Representatives, December 1994. He was later blamed for unnecessarily prolonging the 1995 budget settlement in retaliation for not being allowed to sit at the front of an aircraft with Bill Clinton when they travelled together to the funeral of assassinated Israeli Prime Minister Yitzhak Rabin, November 1995

Which of the two of us do you think cares more about the government not showing up. Him or me?

GINGRICH, provoking a second shutdown of the American federal services because of failure to settle the budget, January 1996

I'll walk naked down Main Street.

JIM WHITAKER, Mayor of North Platte, Nebraska, promising to raise $5,000 for a local animal charity, August 1998. He duly fulfilled his pledge: 'Naked' was a puppy dog. The stunt caused a media storm for the Mayor, with criticism of his demeaning the office of Mayor, then from disappointed citizens taken in by the joke

As to the idea of freezing wages . . . I think this would be monstrously unfair . . . I do not think you could ever legislate for wage increases, and no party is setting out to do that.

HAROLD WILSON, March 1966. Four months later, he introduced a wage freeze

I see no need for a Royal Commission [on trade unions] which would take minutes and waste years.

HAROLD WILSON, September 1964. He announced one six months later

I have often been accused of putting my foot in my mouth, but I have never put my hand in your pocket.

SPIRO AGNEW, Richard Nixon's Vice-President, 1969–73

Ahem . . . I May Have Misled You

Criminal elements . . . are truly the enemies of our country . . . They weaken its economy by infiltrating legitimate businesses . . . by cheating on taxes, and by other frauds. These then are the enemy: the organized criminal . . . the tax cheat, the embezzler . . . the dishonest businessman. Like all who threaten the life and health of the nation, they must be fought with every weapon available.

AGNEW, June 1970. He resigned in 1973 pleading 'no contest' to charges of bribery, extortion and tax fraud involving contracts going back ten years to his time as Governor of Maryland and continuing when he became Vice-President. The court document listing the charges ran to forty pages

After all, what does a politician have but credibility?

AGNEW

When the President does it, that means it is not illegal.

Ex-President NIXON, interview 1988

The President is not above the law. Nor does he contend that he is.

JAMES ST CLAIR, special counsel to President Nixon, Supreme Court argument during the Watergate scandal, July 1974

We intend to play the ball, not the man . . .

HAROLD WILSON, disclaiming interest in who would win the leadership contest in the Conservative Party, October 1963

After half a century of democratic advance, the whole process has ground to a halt with a 14th Earl.

WILSON, playing the man, on the success of Lord Home, October 1963. Home renounced his earldom two days later to become Sir Alec Douglas-Home and become eligible for a seat in the Commons

I suppose Mr Wilson, when you come to think of it, is the 14th Mr Wilson.

LORD HOME, in response

Ahem . . . I May Have Misled You

We destroy these resources at our own peril.

President BILL CLINTON, speech in a Costa Rica national park, 1996. It later emerged that Presidential security staff had insisted that the 350ft route through the rainforest from the main road to the speaking platform be bulldozed and paved so he could be driven right up to the dais

[Cars] pose a mortal threat to the security of every nation.

AL GORE, in his anti-pollution book 'Earth in the Balance', 1992

Here in Motor City, we recognize that cars have done more than fuel our commerce. Cars have freed the American spirit and given us the chance to chase our dreams.

GORE, as Vice-President, campaigning in the 2000 presidential election, speech in Detroit, 1999

Warming will also cause reductions in mountain glaciers and advance the timing of the melt of mountain snow peaks in polar regions.

Omitted sentence in a draft of a report on global warming, from a section crossed out by PHILIP COONEY, chief of staff for the White House Council on Environmental Quality (and former oil-industry lobbyist), whose note says the section was 'straying from research strategy into speculative findings', June 2005

We've had 30 criminal justice acts since 1997; just nine in education. But passing new laws isn't a sign of toughness — it's often a sign of defeat.

DAVID CAMERON, Conservative party leader, writing in the *Guardian*, January 2006

. . . watch this space . . .

7

Moi?

Ambitions Disavowed

No politician ever covets the top job. Heaven forbid. They seek only to serve. Ambition is alien to their natures. However, under intense and unremitting pressure from their friends, and more out of courtesy than desire, some do finally fail to prevent their names going forward. It seems that, from a notionally vast choice of possible candidates, we end up being governed by one or another of a small group whose firm intention it was that the job should never be theirs . . .

I do not think I shall be tempted to quit this agreeable residence . . . the great object of my political career is now achieved.

BENJAMIN DISRAELI, in Paris watching the fall of Sir Robert Peel, Disraeli's arch political foe, December 1845

I declare unequivocally, I will not accept the vice-presidential nomination.

GEORGE BUSH SNR, running for nomination as the Republican presidential candidate, 1980. He lost to Ronald Reagan, and became Reagan's running mate

I could never be Prime Minister. I do my sums with matchsticks.

LORD HOME, 1962

Moi? Ambitions Disavowed

I would rather die than serve under Lloyd George.

LORD CURZON, Asquith's Lord Privy Seal, 4 December 1916, during Lloyd George's manoeuvrings to force Asquith's resignation because of his handling of the First World War. Asquith quit on 5 December; Curzon accepted the post of Lord President of the Council when Lloyd George became Prime Minister on 7 December, and served throughout the six years of the premiership

There is nothing I want so much as an opportunity to retire.

DWIGHT D. EISENHOWER, when allied military commander, 1945

In the strongest language you can command, you may say that I have no political ambitions at all. Make it even stronger than that if you wish.

EISENHOWER, to his press staff, 1945

My decision to remove myself completely from the political scene is definite and positive.

EISENHOWER, ruling himself out of contention for political office, 1948

Under no circumstances will I ask for relief from this assignment in order to seek nomination to public office.

EISENHOWER, 1952, when supreme commander of NATO. Two months later he announced he would stand for the Presidency that year, and won

If I ever show any interest in yielding to persuasion, please call in the psychiatrists, or even better, the sheriff. I feel that there can be no showing made that my duty extends beyond a one-term performance.

EISENHOWER, 1953, shortly after election. He ran for, and won, a second term in 1956

I promise Patricia Ryan Nixon that I will not again seek public office.

RICHARD NIXON to his wife, 1952. Later the same year he was elected as Eisenhower's Vice-President

Moi? Ambitions Disavowed

I say categorically that I have no contemplation at all of being the candidate for anything in 1964, 1966, 1968 or 1972. Anybody who thinks I would be a candidate for anything in any year is off his rocker.

NIXON, 1963. He ran for, and won, the presidential election in 1968, and retained office in the 1972 election

Of all the men running, Richard Nixon is the most dangerous to have as President. I would never work for that man. That man is a disaster.

HENRY KISSINGER, during election campaign, 1968. He served throughout the Nixon presidency, as National Security Adviser and, from 1973, as Secretary of State

I don't think anybody from the South will be nominated [for President] in my lifetime. If so, I don't think he will be elected.

Senator LYNDON BAINES JOHNSON, a Texan, 1958. He became President in 1963 after Kennedy's assassination, and was elected in his own right in 1964

I will never, never trade my Senate seat for the vice-presidency.

JOHNSON, who became John Kennedy's vice-presidential running mate in 1960

The governor has asked me to reiterate what he has said on many occasions – he is not a candidate for President or any other national office.

RONALD REAGAN'S PRESS OFFICER, 1969

The thought of being President frightens me and I do not think I want the job.

REAGAN, Governor of California, 1973

I'd rather bungee jump without the cord.

ROSS PEROT, unsuccessful third candidate in the 1992 presidential election, asked in April 1993 whether he intended to run again in 1996

Moi? Ambitions Disavowed

We have to be responsive to the people who created this party, and they have a strong desire for me to participate . . . I will continue to make whatever sacrifice is necessary.

PEROT, announcing his intention to run as the Reform Party candidate, July 1996

Knowing full well the responsibilities that devolve on a Prime Minister, and how difficult it is to cater to all requirements of a nation and satisfy them, I will not accept the post of Premier even if it is offered me.

MRS SIRIMAVO BANDARANAIKE of Ceylon, 1958. She became the world's first woman Prime Minister in 1960

I can tell you absolutely, certainly, that at the next election, when my term runs out, I am not going to be in the running.

BORIS YELTSIN, ruling himself out of seeking re-election in 1996, June 1992

My departure . . . would be an irresponsible and irreparably mistaken step . . . I am convinced that I can lead this country out of confusion, anxiety and uncertainty.

YELTSIN, announcing his intention to stand for re-election as President, February 1996

My position on the third term is perfectly simple. I said I would not accept a nomination for a third term under any circumstances, meaning of course a third consecutive term.

THEODORE ROOSEVELT, elaborating his decision to enter the 1912 campaign, after his 1904 announcement that he wouldn't go for a third term

No woman in my time will be Prime Minister or Foreign Secretary – not the top jobs. Anyway, I wouldn't want to be Prime Minister. You have to give yourself one hundred per cent.

MARGARET THATCHER, 1969

It will be years before a woman either leads the [Conservative] Party or becomes Prime Minister. I don't see it happening in my time.

THATCHER, June 1974

I don't want to be leader of the party – I'm happy to be in the top dozen.

THATCHER , 1974

At various times in the next twenty or thirty years I think it is reasonable to anticipate that I will be among the leadership of the Labour Party, but as for being leader, I can't see it happening, and I'm not particularly keen on it happening.

NEIL KINNOCK, 1981. He became Leader in October 1983

I have ten more years of active life. I have other ideas for them.

DOUGLAS HURD, Foreign Secretary, ruling himself out when asked if he planned to stand for the Conservative Party leadership, October 1990. The following month he stood

I have made my position clear. I am not going to take part in that process. I think that Mrs Thatcher will lead the Conservative Party into the next election and that she will win it.

MICHAEL HESELTINE, asked whether he would stand in a leadership contest, October 1990

The opinion polls now say that I am best placed to recover those people who have indicated that without a change of leader they will not vote Conservative at the next election . . . Geoffrey Howe's resignation revealed divisions which would not go away without a contest of this sort.

HESELTINE, announcing his candidature for the leadership, November 1990

As far as I am concerned, the opening bat is well played in and will stay there for some years to come.

JOHN MAJOR, ruling himself out of a leadership contest, October 1990

There are no circumstances under which I would stand as an independent.

KEN LIVINGSTONE, March 1998, before he failed to win the Labour Party nomination for the first election for Mayor of London in 2000

I have made it clear again and again that I have no intention of leaving the Labour Party and it is becoming very tiresome that I have to repeat this.

LIVINGSTONE, June 1999

I am staying in the Labour Party. I am dying in the Labour Party.

LIVINGSTONE, July 1999

I can give them a loyalty oath. If Frank [Dobson] or Glenda [Jackson] wins they would make a fine mayor. I would be happy to campaign for either of them.

LIVINGSTONE, November 1999

If I lose, I'm going to work even harder for Glenda or Frank than if I was the candidate, just so I can tell those who doubted my loyalty to go and stick it.

LIVINGSTONE, January 2000, shortly before the internal party ballot for the Labour candidacy

I have concluded that defence of the principle of London's right to govern itself requires that I stand as an independent candidate for London Mayor on May 4.

LIVINGSTONE, announcing his decision to run as an independent, March 2000. He won, and won again in 2004

I am Al Gore and I used to be the next President of the United States.

AL GORE addressing students in Milan, March 2001, after his November 2000 election defeat to George W. Bush

8

Oh!

Sheer Bloody Nerve

'Oh!' is Hansard's notation for MPs' squeals of outrage at a shocking impertinence; but balls, a brass neck, a thick skin and acres of cheek are among the qualifications for high office. Statements which may be downright arrogant, unbelievably insensitive or perfectly preposterous are routine. For brazen effrontery, Catherine the Great takes the biscuit – and runs with it in the relay which follows . . .

I shall be an autocrat: that's my trade. And the good Lord will forgive me: that's his.

CATHERINE II (the Great), Empress of Russia 1762-96 (attrib.)

It's not a day for soundbites, really, we can leave those at home. But I feel the hand of history on our shoulder in respect to this.

TONY BLAIR, press conference, during Northern Ireland Good Friday peace negotiations, April 1998

An extraordinary affair. I gave them their orders and they wanted to stay and discuss them.

DUKE OF WELLINGTON, description of his first Cabinet as Prime Minister, 1828

A statement should also be prepared showing how wise and necessary this was and how what has been achieved justifies me (a) in having created, and (b) in now abolishing the post in question.

Instruction from WINSTON CHURCHILL to the Cabinet Secretary, August 1953, when he decided to abandon his scheme for 'overlords' supervising multiple departments, in this case the post of Secretary of State for the Co-ordination of Transport, Fuel and Power, which he had created just fifteen months earlier

Why has Jesus Christ so far not succeeded in inducing the world to follow his teachings? It is because He taught the ideal without devising any practical means of attaining it. That is why I am proposing a practical scheme to carry out His aims.

President WOODROW WILSON, setting himself modest ambitions for the post-First World War world, Versailles Peace Conference, 1919

All such legal professions demand the utmost discretion, and women are constitutionally incapable of keeping a secret.

French senator M. DUPLANTIER, successfully halting a proposed law that would allow women to become solicitors, March 1932

We went into West Beirut in order to guarantee it, not to control it. We went in to prevent bloodshed, to prevent anarchy.

BEN MEIR, deputy Prime Minister of Israel, on the Israeli invasion of Lebanon in 1982. An estimated 18,000 people died and 30,000 were injured, 90 per cent of them civilians, including over 1,000 in a massacre at two Palestinian refugee camps in the city

From the Israeli point of view, it is the most humane siege of a city imaginable.

IZCHAK BEN-ARI, Israeli ambassador to Germany, on the invasion of Beirut, 1982

It was the right address applied to the wrong building.

US INTELLIGENCE spokesman explaining the mistaken bombing of the Chinese embassy in Belgrade, during NATO air strikes to deter Serbian aggression in Kosovo, May 1999

The Swiss did not say no to Europe. They chose to answer the question later.

EUROPEAN COMMISSION spokesman after a Swiss referendum had rejected joining the EU by a four to one margin, March 2001

Whenever you accept our views, we shall be in full agreement with you.

GENERAL MOSHE DAYAN, Israeli Foreign Minister to US Secretary of State Cyrus Vance during Arab-Israeli peace talks, August 1977

In a sense, the system worked, although it took some time.

DENNIS HAWKINS, Deputy District Attorney for New York, on the case of an innocent man who served eight years in prison before being exonerated

Inflation is not all bad. After all, it has allowed every American to live in a more expensive neighbourhood without moving.

ALAN CRANSTON, California Senator, 1979

Too much democracy leads to homosexuality, moral decay, racial intolerance, economic decline, single-parent families and a lax work ethic.

MAHATHIR MOHAMAD, Malaysia's no-nonsense and longest-serving Prime Minister, April 1998

I am proud of democracy in the country and do not want to do anything against it.

Indian Prime Minister INDIRA GANDHI, July 1975. The previous month she had responded to a High Court ruling declaring her 1971 election null and void by arresting 676 opposition leaders, postponing elections due in 1976, changing the electoral law to nullify the court judgement against her. She then ruled under a national State of Emergency for twenty-one months

Oh! Sheer Bloody Nerve

We're the most democratic country in Latin America.

FIDEL CASTRO, Cuban leader, July 1991

A quantum leap in Iraqi democracy . . . It is a heartfelt referendum, a spiritual one and a principled one.

IZZAT IBRAHIM, Vice-President of Iraq announcing a 100 per cent turnout in a referendum on the continued rule of Saddam Hussein, October 2002, five months before the Allied invasion. Ibrahim further declared that all 11,445,638 ballots had been 'Yes' votes, beating the 99.96 per cent affirmative vote of Saddam's last referendum seven years earlier

Law 5: All repressive laws shall be repealed. Law 6: Drinking, adultery, obscenity, gambling, and other immoral practices shall be banned.

From the manifesto of the Muslim resistance in Afghanistan announcing a list of new laws to be introduced if it defeated occupying Soviet forces, 1981

Vietnam was the first war ever fought without any censorship [of the media]. Without censorship, things can get terribly confused in the public mind.

General WILLIAM WESTMORELAND, US military commander, 1982.

If I was there for several terms of office, it wasn't because I wanted to be. It was because the people insisted.

ALFREDO STROESSNER, Paraguayan dictator accounting for his thirty-five years as President, in which he orchestrated seven fraudulent re-elections, April 1990

At least I left shoes in my closets and not skeletons. And besides, I didn't have 3,000 pairs of shoes. I only had 1,060.

IMELDA MARCOS, 1987

I was never attached to power or valuables. I have no attachment to worldly things.

MARCOS, about to return to the Philippines from exile in Hawaii to face charges that she and her late husband President Ferdinand Marcos salted away $2 billion from the state treasury, October 1991

Oh! Sheer Bloody Nerve

People tell me I live in a mansion here, but I tell them I used to live in a palace. It's all relative.

MARCOS, on life in exile in Hawaii, September 1989

Even Singapore, a country the size of a piece of snot, can swagger around to criticise Taiwan at the United Nations.

CHEN TAN-SUN, Taiwan Foreign Minister's riposte to George Yeo, Singapore's Foreign Minister, whose speech to the UN General Assembly had warned of the dangers to other countries in the region of Taiwan pressing for independence from China, September 2004

You can't trust people who cook as badly as that. After Finland, it's the country with the worst food.

JACQUES CHIRAC, French President, on Britain during the final stages of the two countries' bids to host the 2012 Olympics, July 2005, upsetting the Finns along the way. London won

I don't question your sincerity; don't question my morality. You lose your temper very easily. To be President of the republic, you must remain calm.

NICOLAS SARKOZY to Segolene Royal's attack during a televised debate, May 2007. He won the election. On his first official visit to the United States the following October, he stormed out of a televised interview with the prestigious CBS *60 Minutes* show when asked a question about his troubled marriage. His divorce would be announced two weeks later.

What an imbecile.

SARKOZY berating his press aide as he walked out of *60 Minutes*

Then get lost, you poor jerk.

SARKOZY, February 2008, losing his temper at the Paris agricultural fair while enthusiastically working a line of spectators when one member of the crowd refused to shake hands with him

Oh! Sheer Bloody Nerve

I am the Jesus Christ of politics.

SILVIO BERLUSCONI, Italian Prime Minister, describing himself as a martyr for his nation, election campaign February 2006. He also compared himself to Churchill and Napoleon during the contest

I trust the intelligence of the Italian people too much to think that there are so many pricks around who would vote against their own best interests.

SILVIO BERLUSCONI, then Prime Minister seeking to retain office, 2006 Italian general election. He lost

Italy is now a great country to invest in . . . today we have fewer communists and those who are still there deny having been one. Another reason to invest in Italy is that we have beautiful secretaries . . . superb girls.

BERLUSCONI, while Prime Minister, remarks while visiting the New York Stock Exchange, September 2004

If I, taking care of everyone's interests, also take care of my own, you can't talk about a conflict of interest.

BERLUSCONI, on his alleged conflict of interest as Prime Minister while being one of Italy's biggest media tycoons

The women of the Right are certainly the most beautiful ... the Left has no taste, not even when it comes to women.

BERLUSCONI, during his successful election campaign, April 2008

Zapatero has formed a government that is too pink, something that we cannot do in Italy because there is a prevalence of men in politics and it isn't easy to find women who are qualified.

BERLUSCONI, on the decision by the newly re-elected Spanish Prime Minister in April 2008 to appoint a Cabinet with more women than men. 'Now he's asked for it. He will have problems leading them,' continued Berlusconi

Great things happen in small places. Jesus was born in Bethlehem. Jesses Jackson was born in Greenville.

JESSE JACKSON, campaigning for the US Presidency, March 1988

All the waste in a year from a nuclear power plant can be stored under a desk.

RONALD REAGAN, Presidential election campaign, February 1980

I've lived history. I've made history, and I know I'll have my place in history. That's not egoism.

JOHN DIEFENBAKER, Canadian Prime Minister, January 1973

I was my best successor, but I decided not to succeed myself.

PIERRE TRUDEAU, announcing his resignation as Canadian Prime Minister, February 1984

I'm not trying to compare myself with Roosevelt, but he couldn't walk either.

Wheelchair-bound GEORGE WALLACE, Alabama Governor, during the 1976 US Presidential election campaign

When you are confident about your party, you do not have to prove how Scottish it is.

ALEX SALMOND, leader of the Scottish National Party, September 1998 speech. He proceeded to use the words 'Scots', 'Scottish' or 'Scotland' 95 times

Writers are much more esteemed here; they play a much larger part in society than they do in the West . . . the advantage of not being free is that people do listen to you.

LORD (CP) SNOW, being interviewed on Radio Moscow, 1971

In the case of nutrition and health, just as in the case of education, the gentlemen in Whitehall really do know better what is good for the people than the people know themselves.

DOUGLAS JAY, Labour ideologist and future Labour Treasury and Trade Minister, in *The Socialist Case,* 1937

Illness is a consequence of sin.

Archbishop PAUL CORDES, head of the Vatican agency for humanitarian relief, presenting the Papal message for Lent, February 2002

I took part in the Grunwick picket line . . . I joined in because I thought my union, APEX, was perfectly right on the merits of the dispute.

SHIRLEY WILLIAMS, Paymaster General in the Labour government, 1977

Well, I wasn't part of the picket line. I visited those who were picketing.

WILLIAMS, general election campaign (in which she lost her seat), 1979

Obviously I don't support it, but I support the impulses that are giving rise to it.

PRESIDENT CLINTON, on a Congressional proposal to balance the US budget, 1995

I was not even setting out an argument. I was setting out the facts, the pros and the cons, as dispassionately as I could.

LORD IRVINE, Lord Chancellor, on a letter he had written to the House authorities justifying his request for an immediate shipment of fine art for his official apartment. He was giving evidence to the Commons Public Administration Committee investigating the controversial redecoration of his official accommodation which had cost the taxpayer £650,000, including £59,000 for wallpaper, March 1998

That was not soliciting. It was looking for help.

EDWARD REGAN, Comptroller of New York, when under investigation for soliciting campaign contributions from the financial institutions to which his office gave the state's pension business, October 1988

Oh! Sheer Bloody Nerve

I have expressed a degree of regret that can be equated with an apology.

DES BROWNE, Defence Secretary, nearly apologising for his ministry's public relations disaster in April 2007 after a group of Royal Navy sailors, who had been kidnapped by Iranian forces in the Persian Gulf, were allowed to sell their stories to the tabloid press. The outcry that followed forced Browne to reverse the decision

There is plenty of affordable housing – it is simply occupied by the wrong people . . . The problem in New York is not high rents, but low incomes.

JOHN GILBERT III, New York Landlords' Association President, July 1988

I have been asserting for a year that traffic moves faster in London than in comparable cities. I do not know whether this is true. So far, no one has contradicted the claim.

PETER BOTTOMLEY, Roads Minister, answering a Parliamentary question, 1989

I don't know why people are so rude about caravanners. We never have any trouble with traffic – the jams are always behind us.

MARGARET BECKETT, Leader of the House of Commons, Labour Party conference, September 1999

The way we travel is damaging our towns.

ALAN MEALE, junior environment minister, in a speech April 1999 in Peterborough, delivered moments after being driven the two miles from the railway station to the venue in a stretch limo that did just 17 miles to the gallon

My wife does not like to get her hair blown about.

JOHN PRESCOTT, Deputy Prime Minister, Labour Party conference, September 1999, explaining why he took the 300 yard trip from his Bournemouth hotel to the conference hall by car

I can't take my chauffeur everywhere.

DEREK LAUD, then Conservative candidate for Tottenham, explaining why he had been caught drink driving, general election campaign, 1997

Fewer people smoke and there are fewer candles these days.

TOBY JESSEL, Conservative candidate for Twickenham, justifying fire service cuts, general election campaign, April 1997

[She lives] with her boyfriend, three bastard children and [has] never done a proper job.

DAVID EVANS, Conservative candidate for Welwyn Hatfield on his Labour opponent, Melanie Johnson, at the start of the 1997 general election campaign. She won

I applaud both chambers of the General Assembly for passing this vital measure to bring greater focus on combating the lifestyle issues that are destroying the health of Kentuckians. With this initiative, we are enhancing our efforts to promote a healthy lifestyle for all Kentuckians.

ERNIE FLETCHER, Governor of Kentucky, signing into law his Wellness and Physical Activity Initiative, April 2006. He later courted controversy by insisting on retaining his limo ride from his official mansion to the Governor's Office – a distance of 500ft. A local newspaper added, 'There is a not a river, swamp, nor alligator between them'

'Gabriel criticizes Bush's Neanderthal speech. Losership, not Leadership'

Title of a press statement issued by German Environment Minister, SIGMAR GABRIEL, castigating the stance of the United States on tackling climate change, April 2008. A month earlier, Gabriel was reported to have commandeered a German government jet to fly him solo back to Berlin from holiday in Majorca for a Cabinet meeting. Carbon emission for the trip was estimated to be 44 tons. It was not an isolated episode. Between January and April 2007, he took the same jet seven times, either solo or with a single staff member. He also had the highest car mileage of all chauffeur-driven German ministers, clocking up 55,000 miles in 2007

Oh! Sheer Bloody Nerve

After being notified of the situation and after researching the matter . . . I came to the conclusion that I was not drafted by the A's.

BILL RICHARDSON, New Mexico Governor, November 2005, retracting the biographical detail he had maintained for nearly four decades: that he had been drafted to pitch for the Kansas City Athletics in 1966 before an injury compelled him to bow out of baseball

My counsel tells me there is no controlling legal authority that says there was any violation of any law.

Vice-President AL GORE, wriggling against accusations of campaign finance irregularities, March 1997. He used the circumlocutory phrase no fewer than seven times

[It is] logical that a minister charged with speaking about the fight against pirated goods should have proof of their existence.

Italian Prime Minister SILVIO BERLUSCONI defending his Foreign Minister, Franco Frattini, who had been caught by journalists in Beijing buying a fake Rolex watch hours before attending an EU-China summit at which counterfeiting was on the agenda, October 2003. Frattini admitted he had given way to temptation and bought the watch 'for an absurdly low price'. Worse still, as Italy was President of the EU at the time, Frattini was head of the EU Delegation

It is a social experience for most people. They want to meet the people in the queue.

DAVID MILLS, Chief Executive of the Post Office, claiming that customers were happy with long waits at post offices, September 2004

Our society is in a much better state of repair than it was 15 to 20 years ago.

JACK STRAW, Justice Secretary, March 2008, responding to widespread public anger over an upsurge in juvenile violence which saw 16 teenagers killed in knife crimes in London alone in the first six months of 2008, binge drinking and a rise in alarm at antisocial behaviour

To make matters worse they have elected a foetus as the party leader. I bet a lot of them wish they had not voted against abortion now.

TONY BANKS, Sports Minister, on the election of William Hague as Conservative Party leader, October 1997

The only time you want to see 100 gypsies on your doorstep.

Publicity from MOLE VALLEY DISTRICT COUNCIL promoting a Hungarian gypsy orchestra's visit to Surrey, February 2002

Inflation . . . is currently running at 8.4 per cent.

DENIS HEALEY, Chancellor of the Exchequer, press conference, September 1974, at the start of the general election campaign. The claim was notorious for its inaccuracy: the actual rate was later shown to be 15.6 per cent

People who start things don't often see the end of them – take Moses and the Promised Land.

MARGARET THATCHER, reflecting with characteristic modesty on her premiership, 1992

I want them to have the courage of my convictions.

MARGARET THATCHER, asked by an interviewer whether she respected independent-minded Cabinet colleagues who had the courage of their convictions

The facts. The facts. I have been elected to *change* the facts.

MARGARET THATCHER, shortly after becoming Prime Minister, riposte to her Chief Scientist, Professor John Ashworth, who had countered her rejection of a report on unemployment by saying 'But, it's based on the facts'.

I rate myself a deeply committed pacifist.

RICHARD NIXON, 1971

Oh! Sheer Bloody Nerve

Wherever any . . . father talks to his child, I hope he can look at the man in the White House and, whatever he may think of his politics, he will say: 'Well, there is a man who maintains the kind of standards personally that I would want my child to follow.'

NIXON, TV debate with John Kennedy, presidential campaign, 1960

Let us begin by committing ourselves to the truth, to see it like it is and to tell it like it is, to find the truth, to speak the truth and live with the truth. That's what we'll do.

NIXON, accepting the Republican presidential nomination, 1968

Now the purists probably won't agree with [the break-in], but I don't think you're going to see a great, great uproar in the country.

NIXON, to his aides four days after the Watergate break-in, June 1972, taped conversation released in 1993

The White House has had no involvement whatever in this particular incident.

NIXON, first public comment on the Watergate break-in, five days after the event, June 1972

I don't give a shit what happens. I want you all to stonewall it. Let them plead the Fifth Amendment, cover up, or anything else if it'll save the plan.

NIXON, White House tapes, on obstructing the Watergate investigations, March 1973

There can be no whitewash at the White House.

NIXON, address to the nation after sacking four of his most senior aides whom he sought to make responsible for the Watergate cover-up, April 1973

I reject the cynical view that politics is inevitably or even usually a dirty business.

NIXON, same address, April 1973

I want these to be the best days in American history.

NIXON, concluding the address, referring to the 1,361 days remaining in his presidency, April 1973

Oh! Sheer Bloody Nerve

I am convinced that we are going to make it the whole road and put this thing in the funny pages of the history books.

JOHN DEAN, counsellor to Richard Nixon, reassuring the President on the forthcoming Senate investigation into Watergate, 1973

Watergate is water under the bridge.

RICHARD NIXON, September 1973

I've got what it takes to stay.

NIXON, November 1973

I do not expect to be impeached, and I will not resign.

NIXON, February 1974

I let down my friends. I let down my country. I let down our system of government.

NIXON, 1977

We did not – repeat – did not trade weapons or anything else for hostages – nor will we.

RONALD REAGAN, national TV broadcast, denying allegations of arms sales to Iran in return for the release of American hostages held in Lebanon, 13 November 1986. Six days later he admitted there had been a deal

I did not approve the arms trade.

REAGAN, 11 February 1987

I don't remember – period.

REAGAN, questioned about his involvement, 20 February 1987

I don't recall.

ED MEESE, Attorney General and close Reagan confidant, testifying to the Congressional Iran-Contra hearings, 1987. He used this, or similar phrases, 187 times

Oh! Sheer Bloody Nerve

A few months ago I told the American people I did not trade arms for hostages. My heart and my best intentions still tell me that is true, but the facts and the evidence tell me it is not.

RONALD REAGAN, correcting his earlier denial of involvement in selling arms to Iran in return for the release of American hostages held in Lebanon, March 1987

I'm not worried about the deficit. It is big enough to take care of itself.

RONALD REAGAN, November 1988. His Presidency created the first $100 billion annual budget deficit in American history in 1982 (and its first $200 billion deficit just two years later)

I can assure the House nothing of the kind ever occurred. I never shall – it is totally foreign to my nature – make any application for any place . . . I never directly or indirectly solicited office.

BENJAMIN DISRAELI, lying to the House of Commons, 1846, after his speech criticizing Prime Minister Peel's fitness for office. Peel had immediately retaliated by asking, if that was the case, why Disraeli had asked him for a post in his government. Disraeli had indeed written to Peel in 1841 begging for office. His luck held – Peel could not find the letter to prove it until years later

Son, they're *all* my helicopters.

PRESIDENT JOHNSON, on a visit to a military base, to the officer who had directed him with the words, 'That's your helicopter over there, sir'

Reporter at the Capitol greeting Johnson: Lovely morning.
Johnson: Thank you.

Just calm down, baby.

JOHN CROSBIE, Canadian Minister of Justice, to Sheila Copps, an opposition member during a heated debate in the Canadian House of Commons, 1985. Crosbie was also Minister for the Status of Women at the time

They should've prayed too.

REV. PAT ROBERTSON, religious-right US presidential candidate 1988, reminded of his admission that in 1978 he prayed that an impending hurricane would not hit his television station. It hit somewhere else, and killed several people

The boys have fought for four years . . . they deserve their fun.

STALIN, on reports of mass rape of German women by occupying Russian troops after the end of World War Two, 1945. Up to two million are thought to have been victims

No-one is perfect.

SUSILO BAMBANG YUDHOYONO, President of Indonesia, February 2008, on the death of former dictator Suharto, thought to have been responsible for half a million deaths in suppressing Communist subversion in the 1960s and in his 31 years in power fleecing the Indonesian economy of up to $35 billion through corruption. According to an international anti-corruption group in 2004, Suharto topped the world all-time record for personal graft

Not only do they give you a beautiful face and skin, but they also protect you from disease.

MANTO TSHABALALA-MSIMANG, South African Health Minister, who advocated using garlic and lemon rind as AIDS treatments and warned against antiretroviral drugs because of dangerous side effects, May 2005

I was elected by a bunch of fat, stupid, ugly old ladies that watch soap operas, play bingo, read tabloids and don't know the metric system.

TOM ALCIERE, on his election as a Republican member of the New Hampshire state legislature, November 2000. His unorthodox take on authority emerged within days when he said that he believed police officers deserved to be killed ('Nobody will ever be safe until the last cop is dead.') and that women needed to be 'dragged by the hair and either threatened with a bat or hit with a bat once in a while'. He was forced to resign within two months

Oh! Sheer Bloody Nerve

Sir Peter Tapsell MP is in your street. If you'd like to meet him, present yourself at your front door.

Loud hailer announcement from Sir Peter's landrover parading sedately down streets in his East Midlands seat of Louth and Horncastle. The MP was widely regarded as the last of the patrician breed of Tory member. He held his seat in the election, and remains the MP as of the date of publication

Blah!

Written answer given by JIM MATHER, Enterprise Minister in the devolved Scottish government, to a parliamentary question about drug use in Scottish prisons

People say I'm arrogant, but I know better.

JOHN SUNUNU, Chief of Staff in the Bush Snr White House, 1991

Advice to politicians: Always be sincere, whether you mean it or not.

CHARLES PERCY, US Senator for Illinois, 1976

Look, we are not making empty promises. This is a blueprint to create heaven on earth.

PETER WARBURTON, deputy leader of the Natural Law Party, general election manifesto launch 1997

Sir Ivan has appeared in many famous trials, including the Christine Keeler and *Fanny Hill* cases. He also acted for the defence of the Kray twins, serial killer Dennis Neilson, the Brighton Babes in the Woods murders and the Brinks Matt gold bullion robbery.

SIR IVAN LAWRENCE QC, convincing voters in Burton of his trustworthiness, general election campaign, April 1997. His attempt was unsuccessful – Labour won the seat

Oh! Sheer Bloody Nerve

There's a candidate in this race who was actually convicted of a crime, and it's not me.

Republican Massachusetts Senate aspirant JACK E ROBINSON III, challenging Edward Kennedy in the 2000 election. In an unorthodox approach to honesty, he published an 11-page mea culpa of all his previous transgressions, which included sexual assault, drink-driving offences, plagiarism and drug-taking. But none involved criminal conviction, unlike Kennedy's record. Within days, the Republicans dropped him. He later also lost bids for Massachusetts Secretary of State in 2002, and for a seat in the US House of Representatives in 2006

We used to have a pint at every stop – the driver's mate did – and we used to have about ten stops in a day. You worked so hard you didn't feel you'd drunk ten pints by four o'clock . . . It's probably horrifying but we used to do that, go home for tea and go out in the evening to the pub.

Conservative leader, WILLIAM HAGUE, recounting in August 2000 his teenage years as a beer delivery mate. The 14-pint a day drinking record was universally ridiculed by commentators. Journalists who tracked down the pub he used to frequent quoted an assistant manager's response: 'That lying little toad . . . some of the old boys have been coming in here for donkey's years and no one can remember Hague coming in for as much as half a lager'

Unlike other candidates, I'm not going to hide my evil side.

JONATHON ('THE IMPALER') SHARKEY, former pro wrestler and candidate for Minnesota Governor, whose platform included a plan to impale terrorists, January 2006. He failed in his election bid

Why should Ontario pay for Quebec's f**king?

Forthright observation of GEORGE DREW, Premier of Ontario, during a parliamentary debate on family allowances, 1975. The birth rate for Protestant Ontario was significantly lower than that of Catholic Quebec

I am busier than a whore working two beds.

C. P. HOWE, Canadian Minister of Trade and Commerce, September 1988

Oh! Sheer Bloody Nerve

The difference between rape and seduction is salesmanship.

BILL CARPENTER, Mayor of Independence, Missouri, 1990

How on earth do you know an advance is unwanted until you've made it?

ALAN CLARK, notorious philandering MP and diarist, to a journalist who asked how he justified 'making unsolicited and unwanted advances to women'

It's like the weather. If it's inevitable, just relax and enjoy it.

CLAYTON WILLIAMS, gaffe-riddled and celebrated bad taste Republican candidate for Governor of Texas, when asked by reporters for his views on rape, April 1990. He didn't win the governorship

You can't have a race living here for 70,000 years without leaving some of their debris about. In another 70,000 years you will be able to see our beer cans, won't you, as a sign of our culture.

AUSTRALIAN MINISTER FOR CONSERVATION, on Aboriginal artefacts, 1981

I'm saying maybe you put them on TV and cut off a thumb.

OSCAR GOODMAN, Las Vegas mayor, in a televised interview November 2005, on how to stop graffiti artists from defacing the city's freeways

If you wanted to reduce crime you could – if that were your sole purpose – you could abort every black baby in this country, and your crime rate would go down.

WILLIAM BENNETT, former US Education Secretary, now a syndicated talk-show host, October 2005. He added that it would be an 'impossible, ridiculous and morally reprehensible thing to do, but your crime rate would go down'

Controlled Immigration . . . Not Chaos and Inhumanity.

New slogans doctored onto 2005 election publicity photos of Dorset South Conservative candidate ED MATTS holding placards with Ann Widdecombe at a demonstration. The original photograph had been taken at a protest Matts had led in favour of an asylum seeking Malawian family, with the placards reading 'Let Them Stay'

Everyone in politics ought to be arrested at least once. It's an education.

ALAN CLARK, after being arrested in Piccadilly for allegedly trying to drive his Land Rover through a police cordon

I think and hope that we have conveyed not merely the impression, but the conviction that, whatever other countries or governments may do, the British government is never untrue to its word, and is never disloyal to its colleagues or its allies, never does anything underhand or mean; and if this conviction be widespread – as I believe it to be – that is the real basis of the moral authority which the British Empire has long exerted and I believe will long continue to exert in the affairs of mankind.

LORD CURZON, Foreign Secretary, 1923

I think sometimes our difficulties with our friends abroad result from our natural good manners and reticence. We are apt not to press our points too strongly in the early stages of a negotiation, and then when a crisis arises and we have to make a definite position we are accused of perfidy.

Prime Minister HAROLD MACMILLAN, note to his Chancellor and Foreign Secretary, June 1958, explaining why Britain's alternative plan to the European Community, the European Free Trade Association, had failed to catch on

I would say the best moment of all was when I caught a seven and a half pound perch in my lake.

GEORGE W. BUSH, answering a German newspaper reporter who asked him to name the best moment of his five years as President, May 2006

Oh! Sheer Bloody Nerve

For the purpose of making a declaration under this Subdivision, the Commissioner may:
a) treat a particular event that actually happened as not having happened; and
b) treat a particular event that did not actually happen as having happened and, if appropriate, treat the event as:
   i) having happened at a particular time; and
   ii) having involved particular action by a particular entity; and
c) treat a particular event that actually happened as:
   i) having happened at a time different from the time it actually happened; or
   ii) having involved particular action by a particular entity (whether or not the event actually involved any action by that entity).

Goods and Services law, AUSTRALIAN TAXATIONS OFFICE, 2005

I murdered my grandmother this morning.

FRANKLIN D. ROOSEVELT, US President 1933–45, habitual comment to White House press reporters if he suspected they were not paying attention

9

Uh?

You Cannot Be Serious

Beneath the daily ebb and flow of opinion, fortune and political fashion, there are more powerful currents at work. Historic shifts are as gradual as they are finally huge, leaving the certainties of other ages looking astonishingly idiotic. But it is important to remember that, though some of the opinions expressed below – were controversial even at the time, few will have seemed absurd. The arguments which follow are from past Members of Parliament as recorded by Hansard. Impossible though it would be to advance them seriously at a modern dinner party, you may react to a few with a sneaking sympathy. You may even sympathize with a few of our ancestors' forebodings about the likely consequences of new inventions. While laughing at what they thought, ask yourself at which of our own assumptions our successors may laugh . . .

The slave trade

It is absurd to suppose that the merchants whose profit arises from the number of healthy Africans they land in the West India islands would not attend to their own interests and take every possible care to preserve their health.

LORD RODNEY, 1788

[Abolition] will terminate all spirit of adventure, all incitement to industry, all thirst of emulation, for hitherto it has been the hope of overseers to rise in the world as soon as they had obtained that employment, and the means they had of doing so was by saving a portion of their wages to purchase two or three Negroes which they let out . . . for hire.

Sɪʀ Wɪʟʟɪᴀᴍ Yᴏᴜɴɢ, 1796

The slave trade [has] promote[d] the cause of humanity, for it can hardly be doubted that . . . prisoners would have shared the same fate as the other [dead warriors] if avarice had not prevailed over revenge in the mind of the savage king.

Mʀ Eᴅᴡᴀʀᴅs, citing the practice of African kings selling prisoners of war to slave traders instead of imposing the usual fate of execution, 1798

The slave trade tends in a very considerable degree to lessen this waste of human blood . . . [slaves] are conveyed from a country of barbarous superstition to a land of civilization and humanity. In my opinion, therefore, the clamours against the trade are groundless.

Mʀ Hᴇɴɴɪᴋᴇʀ-Mᴀᴊᴏʀ, 1798

The Africans are accustomed to slavery in their own country and the taking of them to another quarter of the globe is therefore no great hardship.

Sɪʀ Wɪʟʟɪᴀᴍ Yᴏᴜɴɢ, 1804

The state of slaves in Africa is truly deplorable and therefore taking them away, particularly to the English colonies, is a relief to them.

Mʀ Fᴜʟʟᴇʀ, 1804

❖

With regard to the emancipation of the slaves, I have only to say that the opinion of those who have the best local information on the subject is that such a measure would produce the downfall of the Empire.

Gᴇɴᴇʀᴀʟ Gᴀsᴄᴏʏɴᴇ, 1807

Child labour

[Such intervention] is an imputation on the feelings of parents to suppose that they would suffer their children to work to the prejudice of their health; and it is also an imputation on gentlemen at the head of manufactories to suppose that they would compel children to make excessive exertions.

Mr Curwen, opposing plans for government to legislate on the hours children could work in factories, 1816

At present parents find a difficulty in bringing [children] up well even by the united produce of their labour. The difficulty will be much greater when the children themselves are prevented from contributing anything towards their own support.

Lord Stanley, on the first Factory Act limiting the hours of child labour, 1818

Limiting the hours of labour cannot tend to improve [morals]. On the contrary, it will only give more opportunities for idleness and all the bad consequences arising from it.

Lord Stanley, 1818

I object [to limiting child labour] but so far from considering myself an enemy of the children . . . I reckon myself their friend [since] they are improved in health, number and comfort by the free disposal of their labour. If their hours of working are reduced, their wages likewise must be reduced and then they might be exposed to the hardships of want . . . Under the present system the children have labour, food and clothing, under the proposed one they will have idleness, poverty and wretchedness.

Earl of Rosslyn, 1819

Will morals be improved as degrading poverty advances? Will education spread when wages become lower? Will manners become more civilized and will religion penetrate the masses when discontent has taken the place of prosperity and when ease and comfort have given place to despair?

Sir James Graham, Home Secretary, opposing restrictions on child labour, 1844

Education

To carry the system of education to the labouring poor . . . will . . . raise their minds above their lot in life and by no means strengthen their attachments to those laborious pursuits by which they are to earn a livelihood.

GEORGE ROSE, vice-president of the Board of Trade, 1807

I do not think . . . that the occupiers of lands and houses should be taxed in order that all the children in the country should be taught to read and write, especially when it is doubtful whether writing will be of any real use.

NICHOLAS VANSITTART, secretary of the Treasury, 1807

[Education for the poor] is more pregnant with mischief than advantage . . . it will teach [the poor] to despise their lot in life instead of making them good servants in agriculture and other laborious employments to which their rank in society has destined them. Instead of teaching them subordination, it will render them factious and refractory [and] insolent to their superiors.

MR GIDDY, 1807

It is a good people and not a gabbling people that is wanted in the country, and this smattering of education will only raise the labourers of this country above the situations best suited to their own interests . . . It will put into their heads that they were not born to labour but to get their living without it.

WILLIAM COBBETT, 1834

I do not believe . . . it will be possible if desirable, or desirable if possible, to establish a system of compulsory education in this country.

LORD BROUGHAM, 1837

To give education gratuitously will only degrade the education so given in the estimation of the parents.

LORD ROBERT MONTAGU, opposing free education, 1870

It would be a very dangerous thing for us to . . . take upon ourselves as the state the burden of the education of the children of any portion of the population . . . We would in effect say to the great body of parents throughout the country, 'We think it our business rather than yours to educate your children,' and I do not think we would be serving the cause of education by allowing such a belief . . .

WILLIAM FORSTER, vice-president of the Council and minister responsible for education, piloting his Education Act of 1870

I consider it a most dangerous thing to convert a nation of labourers into a nation of clerks.

MR SANDFORD, 1876

It has been said that children should be kept at school until fourteen years of age; but the amount and importance of the labour which lads between ten and fourteen can perform should not be ignored. Since the present educational system has come into operation, the weeds have very much multiplied in Norfolk which was once regarded as quite the garden of England, weeding being particularly the work of children whose labour is cheap, whose sight is keen, bodies flexible and fingers nimble.

EARL FORTESCUE, 1880

Parliamentary reform

I do not think it would be politic or for the interest of the country to have this House quite subject to popular control.

GEORGE CANNING, former Foreign Secretary, and Prime Minister to be, 1810

What the present composition of parliament enables us to do is ... to separate the real permanent sense of the people from their hasty passing impressions and to keep up that right of appeal from present passion to future judgement which is necessary in order to preserve us from all the horrors and absurdities of democratic government.

MR WARD, on the pre-reformed system which gave the vote to 3 per cent of the population, 1812

It would soon become the base pander of the basest passions of the people.

MR GIDDY, 1812, on a democratically elected Commons

I am decidedly for opposing the beginning of a system which must end in national destruction. [It is] pregnant with the most fatal consequences.

GEORGE CANNING, 1817

Under such a system, all who have the real and permanent good of their country at heart must tremble for its future state ... democratic reform will lead on to a state of anarchy, confusion and ruin and inflict the most serious evils upon all classes of society from the peasant in his cottage to the king on his throne.

MR TREVOR, opposing the Reform Bill, 1832

It is my belief that every general election under such circumstances must be attended with serious riots in all parts of the metropolis.

SIR RICHARD VYVYAN, 1832

❖

The education fitting a man to decide on the important interests and mighty questions involved in the government of a great nation can never be acquired by those who, because they are earning their daily bread by daily toil, can never possess the leisure for study or for thought.

EARL OF HARROWBY, 1852

I doubt very much whether a democracy is a government that would suit this country.

BENJAMIN DISRAELI, 1865

[The result of widening the franchise would be] a Parliament of no statesmanship, no eloquence, no learning, no genius. Instead of these, you will have a horde of selfish and obscure mediocrities, incapable of anything but mischief . . . devised and regulated by the raging demagogue of the hour.

DISRAELI, opposing reform, 1866. As Chancellor and Leader of the Commons, he piloted through the Reform Bill giving the vote to working-class householders the following year

Voting is not a right; voting is a public function. No one has any more right to be a voter than he has to be . . . a policeman, or a judge, or Prime Minister.

LORD CECIL, House of Lords, 1931

Secret voting

With the feelings of an Englishman, I protest against this secret and unmanly mode of voting . . . I do not think that any public benefit can arise from this change . . . Is it desirable that men should make a promise with one hand and break it with the other?

EARL OF DARLINGTON, opposing secret voting, 1833

[The] first effect will infallibly be an organized system of spies to ascertain whether persons voted according to their promises which will create heart-burnings and jealousies among the lower classes that must put an end to all social peace and comfort.

VISCOUNT HOWICK, 1835

I object to it because I think it at variance with the national character . . . I think a true Englishman hates doing a thing in secret or in the dark. I do not believe that a majority of Englishmen would consent to give their votes in secret even if the law permitted them to do so . . . I say that for men who are charged with the high and important duty of choosing the best men to represent the country in Parliament to go sneaking to the ballot-box, and, poking in a piece of paper, looking round to see that no one could read it, is a course which is unconstitutional and unworthy of the character of straightforward and honest Englishmen.

LORD PALMERSTON, former Foreign Secretary and Prime Minister to be, address to his electors at the general election, 1852

Life peerages

I very much doubt whether many persons will be found to seek for the honour of a life peerage, for it seems to me that it would amount I will not say to an insult but to a very humiliating slight to offer a gentleman a peerage and at the same time to tell him that the title and dignity conferred upon him shall not descend to his son.

EARL OF MALMESBURY, on the first plan to introduce life peers, 1869. They would not be introduced until 1958

I do not believe that . . . representatives of the [commercial or industrial] interests would be willing in any large number to accept seats in this House for they would come in upon a different footing from those among whom they sat and accordingly would feel the position more or less a position of degradation.

EARL OF HARROWBY, 1869

What I fear is this, that you will not strengthen the House of Lords as a legislative body but that you will turn it into a sort of legislative Bath or Cheltenham or perhaps . . . into a sort of legislative hydropathic establishment where these noble persons will take more care of their constitutions than of the constitution of this House.

EARL OF ROSEBERY, leader of the Opposition in House of Lords, 1888

I have no idea of the kind of persons we are going to get as life peers. I am sceptical about whether we are going to get anybody worthwhile at all.

LORD SILKIN, deputy leader of the Opposition in House of Lords, 1957

Members [of the House of Commons] are, of course, delighted at the thought [of life peerages] because they can elevate their more rumbustious female elements to this House. I hate the idea of your Lordships' House becoming a repository for over-exuberant female politicians and unfortunately we are unable to elevate them further, for that Prerogative rests with the Almighty.

EARL FERRERS, 1957

Votes for women

[Women's] vocation is a high one. Their vocation is to make life endurable.

MR SCOURFIELD, 1870

It is not a disability that women should not have a vote but it is rather a privilege that they should not be mixed up in political strife.

MR FOWLER, 1870

Reason predominates in the man, emotion and sympathy in the woman and if the female vote makes any noticeable difference in the character of our constituencies the risk is that we will have in the House an excess of the emotional and sentimental element over the logical and reasoning faculty.

MR BERESFORD HOPE, 1871

Our legislation will develop hysterical and spasmodic features.

MR BERESFORD HOPE, 1871

We regard woman as something to admire, to reverence, to love; and while we will share with her the happiness of life, we will shield her as far as possible from its harsher and sterner duties . . . We will not be parties to dragging her down into the arena of our everyday toil and strife.

EDWARD KNATCHBULL-HUGESSEN, under-secretary for the colonies, 1872

It [is] the business of the man to do the hard work and of the woman to make [the] home bright and cheerful for him.

MR BOUVERIE, 1872

The real fact is that man in the beginning was ordained to rule over the woman, and this is an eternal decree which we have no right and no power to alter.

DUKE OF NORTHUMBERLAND, 1873

All the advantages women possess they obtain by reason of their weakness.

MR HANBURY, House of Commons, 1878

Women can gain nothing but they will be likely to lose a great deal . . . Fancy a Member returning home . . . and finding there a politician in petticoats ready to continue the debate! . . . [It will result in] a system that will eventually destroy the home.

HENRY RAIKES, 1879

There are certain ladies of very great intellect, no doubt they are women by accident and they want to assume the position of men.

Now I object to legislating for what, with all respect to the ladies, I may call freaks of nature.

HENRY LABOUCHERE, 1891

Intellectually women have not the gifts which fit them for being elected. They have got a certain amount of what I might call instinct rather than reason [and] they are impulsive, emotional and have got absolutely no sense of proportion.

LABOUCHERE, 1897

I do not know how domestic bliss is to be continued if a man is perpetually leaving his own wife and visiting another man's wife on the plea that he wanted [her vote]. I think that [the House] would agree with me that that would be a very dangerous state of things.

LABOUCHERE, 1904

I think it might fairly be said that women cannot fulfil the duties of citizenship. Of course, it is not their fault that they are more beautiful than muscular.

LABOUCHERE, House of Commons, 1905

Women have at present such an influence over the actions of men that if they had been really united on the desire for the franchise they would have got it long ago. It is only a few women with masculine minds who take an interest in politics and desire to have votes.

LABOUCHERE, 1905

I am quite certain that if women are introduced into the House it would be useless to debate any point at all because the women will have made up their minds before the debate begins.

SIR FREDERICK BANBURY, 1905

Sensible and responsible women do not want to vote. The relative positions to be assumed by men and women in the working out of our civilization were assigned long ago by a higher intelligence than ours.

GROVER CLEVELAND, former US President, 1905

You will never . . . persuade the English nation to take a step which would result in a majority of voters being women.

MR HARWOOD, House of Commons, 1910

Does this country really want to see a mixed House of Commons composed of men and women? . . . this must be the natural consequence of giving women the vote . . . and if they become Members they are bound to become ministers . . . Is it really possible that we should contemplate making such a spectacle of ourselves to the civilized world?

MR BURDETT-COUTTS, 1911

There are obvious disadvantages about having women in Parliament. I do not know what is going to be done about their hats . . . How is a poor little man to get on with a couple of women wearing enormous hats in front of him?

MR HUNT, 1913

I know that the ladies are far cleverer than the men in certain relations of life; but government does not require cleverness; it requires wisdom and judgement and we do not so much expect wisdom and judgement from the ladies as enthusiasm in the pursuit of what they consider right.

LORD CLIFFORD OF CHUDLEIGH, 1928

Income Tax

This burden should not be left to rest on the shoulders of the public in time of peace because it should be reserved for the important occasions which, I trust, will not soon recur.

HENRY ADDINGTON, Prime Minister and Chancellor of the Exchequer, abolishing income tax, 1802.

The nation has so unequivocally expressed their indignation at the degrading and oppressive nature of the tax that I am sure no minister will ever dare to reinflict it on the country.

MR JONES, on the abolition of income tax, 1802. It was revived the following year.

Old Age Pensions

Any universal scheme for giving pensions to everybody is . . . beyond the resources of the state. It would cost such an enormous sum and would involve such an entire disintegration of our whole financial system that it is perfectly impossible to contemplate it as practical legislation.

JOSEPH CHAMBERLAIN, Colonial Secretary, 1899

If . . . we say to any workman, 'Drink away as much as you like for when you grow old you shall be supported in comfort at the expense of your colleagues who have not drunk,' then clearly we are subsidizing drunkenness.

MR COX, 1907

In my opinion, pensions . . . are worse than a waste of public money; they are the greatest possible incentive to the absence of self-reliance and thrift.

VISCOUNT ST ALDWYN, 1907

Holidays

If the House enforces idleness by Act of Parliament on the working classes of this country, we will be initiating a ruinous principle which will tend still further to give the advantages which foreign countries are now obtaining over us in all our great national industries for which, up to this time, this country has been pre-eminent.

MR WILSON, opposing Bank Holidays, 1875

Decimal currency

If you imposed the decimal coinage in this country, you would have a revolution within a week.

HERBERT ASQUITH, Prime Minister, at the Imperial conference, 1911

Motor Cars

We grow corn, oats, hay and straw. Motors do not eat oats, they do not eat hay and they do not lie on the straw and when horses are done away with, it will not be worth while our growing these agricultural articles of consumption having lost our best customer.

EARL OF WEMYSS, 1903

Depend upon it, if these motorists and motor cars are not kept in order they will have to leave the roads altogether because in the long run the people will never submit to the intolerable nuisance which has been created.

MR CRIPPS, 1903

I do not believe the introduction of motor cars will ever affect the riding of horses; the prophecies that have been made are likely to be falsified as have been those made when the railways were introduced.

MR SCOTT-MONTAGU, 1903

Uh? You Cannot Be Serious

If the use of the horn or warning signal by motorists was forbidden ... they would have to go much slower ... and would not be able, by blowing a horn, to order everybody else out of the way. Their speed would be greatly reduced, they would have to pull up oftener and they would be forced to be a little more considerate of other people.

LORD WILLOUGHBY DE BROKE, proposing the banning of horns on cars as the solution to speeding, 1908

I am not one of those people who believe that speed *per se* is really going to make for dangerous driving on our roads today ... I do not believe the retention of the speed limit will really have any effect in helping to reduce the number of accidents.

LORD ERSKINE, supporting a government-inspired Bill to abolish the speed limit for cars, 1930. The limits were reintroduced four years later after a big increase in accidents

We must make the motorist feel that when he is discourteous and inconsiderate on the road he is not a British gentleman, and that we are not going to regard him as such.

HERBERT MORRISON, Minister of Transport, piloting the 1930 abolition Bill

To those who suggest that it is an unreasonable hardship to motorists not to drive above thirty miles an hour in a populated area, I would reply that a careful driver has no pleasure in going faster than that.

MR ANSTRUTHER-GRAY, on the Bill to reintroduce speed limits, 1934

I firmly believe that a time is coming when many of the problems we are discussing today are going to solve themselves automatically with quickened reaction, with inherited caution, when an ingrained sense of safety is going to take the place of many of these restrictions and regulations which we now have to impose.

OLIVER STANLEY, Minister of Transport, in charge of the 1934 Bill

211

My own view is . . . that ultimately we shall have to ration cars. We shall have to have a waiting list and people who want motor cars will have to wait for their turn . . . Short of some such method . . . I see great difficulties ahead.

Mr Lovat-Fraser, on road congestion, 1935. (At the time there were 224,000 cars; by the start of the 1990s there were twenty *million* and still no rationing.)

Driving tests

Any advantage which at first sight might appear likely to result from the institution of tests . . . would be outweighed by the expense, difficulties and disadvantages inseparable from any such system.

Colonel Ashley, government roads minister, 1925

My own belief is that the more skilful a man is, the more dangerous he is because he takes greater risks. What really is wanted is road sense and you will not get that by having examinations.

Lord Banbury, 1929

We are satisfied that driving tests have absolutely no value.

Earl Russell, government roads spokesman, House of Lords, 1929

Pedestrian crossings

I do not think it would be practicable to introduce such a system in London.

Colonel Ashley, 1928

[Belisha beacon crossings] are a veritable danger . . . A pedestrian standing by one of them can of course see the beacon and also thinks that the driver of an oncoming vehicle can see it as well. He cannot but the result is that the pedestrian ventures on to the road . . . and an accident is the result. These beacons therefore instead of increasing the safety of pedestrians will definitely do exactly the reverse.

SIR WILLIAM BRASS, 1934

The military

The spectacle of a regiment of motor cars charging, no doubt would be inspiriting but I do not think such a scheme will be likely to prove any permanent advantage to the army.

LORD STANLEY, financial secretary to the War Office, House of Commons, opposing mechanized military transport, 1901

Ordinary common sense tells us that such machines will probably never be used for the carrying of large bodies of troops and ammunition.

SIR GILBERT PARKER, House of Commons, 1909 on mechanized military transport

I doubt whether at any time the reduction of horses will be as great as one might anticipate. I take it that under no circumstances shall we ever want less than 40,000 for the Expeditionary Forces.

LT-COL JOHN SEELY, under-secretary, War Office, House of Commons, 1911. (He became Secretary of State for War the following year.)

I believe that [the War Ministry] are entirely wrong in thinking that they can substitute tanks for cavalry . . . That seems to me to be a most extraordinary misreading of the lessons of the war . . . It would be the most extraordinary misconception of the truth to imagine that in applying science to war the first thing to get rid of is the horse. On the contrary, every advance in science has made the horse a more and more indispensable weapon of war. Heavy-artillery fire, heavy-machine-gun fire, gas, aeroplane observation — all these make rapid movement more essential.

JOHN SEELY, former Secretary of State for War, House of Commons, 1921

It is obvious that a tank making a very great noise will give many opportunities to the enemy to conceal themselves. It is quite impossible for tanks to be used with advantage in such terrain as marshy ground or for crossing a river when the bridges have been blown up.

CAPTAIN HOLT, House of Commons, 1926

The cavalry will be able to come into their own when mechanical vehicles have all broken down . . . and when possibly the petrol dumps are all exploded.

BRIGADIER-GENERAL MAKINS MP, House of Commons, 1933

I have had occasion during the past year to study military affairs . . . and the more I study them, the more I am impressed by the importance of cavalry in modern warfare.

ALFRED DUFF COOPER, financial secretary to the War Office, presenting the Army Estimates, House of Commons, March 1934. He was promoted to Secretary of State for War the following year, a post he held until 1937

I am perfectly convinced that the role of the cavalry is still as important today as it has been throughout the ages.

MAJOR SHAW, House of Commons, 1936

Military aviation

I do not think that nations in the future are going to conduct their battles by scattering explosives over houses. That is very unlikely to take place . . . It is entirely contrary to all practice to scatter explosives in the way suggested and that such a brutal and futile proceeding would be resorted to is one which we need not contemplate.

ALFRED MOND, House of Commons, 1909

It will be possible in another war for London to be wrecked by aircraft attack in twelve hours.

MR HUDSON, House of Commons, 1925

The next war is bound to be a short war. I cannot conceive of any country being able to continue a war for a week after its air force, its aerodromes and its petrol tanks have been destroyed . . . The war will be decided . . . not in five years, or in five weeks but in five days.

COLONEL JOSIAH WEDGWOOD, House of Commons, 1934

Broadcasting

Make no mistake about it, the repercussions of this new invention [television] are going to be . . . very wholesome because they tend to keep the home together . . . It does mean that people stay at home.

LORD BRABAZON OF TARA, 1950

With the coming of television [the average youth] now stays indoors three or four nights a week. Those who are worried about the problem of growing juvenile delinquency should take some comfort from the fact that here is a medium which can attract the young.

JOHN RODGERS, Conservative member for Sevenoaks (making him Winston Churchill's MP), 1953

In my view a spate of mediocre entertainment will encourage vacuity and increased vacuity will result in the demand for even more mediocre entertainment – and so on until the jungle finally closes in . . . I feel sure that if this Bill becomes law future historians will deem it to be one of the most irresponsible measures of modern times.

LORD STRABOLGI, opposing commercial television, 1954

This is an age of mass perception and through various media of public communication such as elements of the press, a considerable amount of corruption of consciousness has already taken place; and commercial television will just about sink the ship . . . A nation fed on this pap for one generation might as well scrap its educational system and spend the money on asylums.

LORD NOEL-BUXTON, 1954

I will never reconsider it. It would be shocking to have debates in this House forestalled time after time by expressions of opinion by persons who had not the status or responsibility of Members of Parliament.

SIR WINSTON CHURCHILL, opposing the broadcasting of Parliament, 1955

It would be highly undesirable for [the BBC] to become a simultaneous debating arena with Parliament. There should be explanation, debate, controversy before, and possibly after, Parliament has dealt with an issue but Parliament is the only grand forum of the nation. Once the matter at issue is under actual discussion there, it should not also be being contested on the ether.

CHARLES HILL, Postmaster-General, and government broadcasting minister, quoting the words in 1949 of the BBC's own director-general, 1955

A national disaster.

Labour Party pamphlet, *Challenge to Britain*, giving the party's official view on commercial television before its introduction in 1955

An enemy of reasonable culture.

HERBERT MORRISON, Labour elder statesman, on commercial television

Uh? You Cannot Be Serious

What a total nonsense this business about an image is.

Sir Alec Douglas-Home, on television, resignation speech to Conservative Party conference, 1965

I am a fan of television as far as sport and ceremonial are concerned. I think it less suited to politics than to anything else. You are dealing with the most complicated issues in a very short time and it is bound to be superficial.

Lord Home, 1988

Civil aviation

The task of fostering civilian aviation in the British Isles will be attended with much difficulty. The fogs and mists and other climatic conditions are a terrible hindrance. Moreover, the country is covered by a network of railways and roads which constitute a most formidable competition with the air . . . I should not expect to see a very large or a very rapid development of domestic civil aviation within these islands.

Winston Churchill, Secretary of State for Air, 1921

I do not believe that civil aviation has more than very limited potentialities. I believe it may be made a luxurious and costly mode of travel for a very few rich people. I do not believe it will be able to be brought into use for general transport . . . I believe the aeroplane has little or only a very limited future, the whole of its potentialities are warlike.

Mr Rose, 1923

We in this island shall never fly commercially for more than sixty miles over the island. It will never pay us to fly from London to Glasgow commercially and so all our commercial flying has to be from London to the Channel or from London to the North Sea and then over Europe.

Major Hills, 1928

Civil aviation will never be a commercial proposition in this country. It may be that individuals will continue to use aeroplanes for business and pleasure purposes to an increasing degree but as a commercial proposition I think we are already too well served by our railways.

CAPTAIN CAZALET, 1931

We follow with interest any work that is being done in other countries on jet propulsion, but scientific investigation into the possibilities has given no indication that this method can be a serious competitor to the airscrew-engine combination. We do not consider we should be justified in spending any time or money on it ourselves.

Reply from the AIR MINISTRY to the British Interplanetary Society, 1934

Suez Canal

It is an undertaking which I believe in point of commercial character may be deemed to rank among the many bubble schemes that from time to time have been palmed upon gullible capitalists.

LORD PALMERSTON, Prime Minister, on plans to build the Suez Canal, 1857

The project for executing a canal across the Isthmus of Suez is a most futile idea – totally impossible to be carried out. It will be attended with a lavish expenditure of money for which there will be no return; and even if successfully carried out in the first instance, the operation of nature will in short time defeat the ingenuity of man.

BENJAMIN DISRAELI, Chancellor of the Exchequer, on the building of the Suez Canal, 1858. It opened in 1869 and six years later Disraeli spent £4 million to buy the Egyptian government's shares in it

It is very much regretted . . . that when [England] needs cotton, 30,000 or 40,000 people who might be usefully employed in the cultivation of cotton in Egypt are occupied in digging a canal through a sandy desert . . . I should hope that so useless an occupation will soon be put an end to.

LORD PALMERSTON, Prime Minister, 1864

Science

I am tired of this sort of thing called science. We have spent millions in that sort of thing for the last few years, and it is time it should be stopped.

SIMON CAMERON, US senator for Pennsylvania, opposing funds for the Smithsonian Institution, 1861

Everything that can be invented has been invented.

CHARLES DUELL, US Patent Office addressing President William McKinley to abolish the office, 1899

10

Ouch!

Sitting Ducks

They asked for it . . .

When Napoleon retreated from Moscow after his failed invasion of Russia in 1812, he fled almost alone leaving his army to fend for itself. On reaching the Neman river:

Napoleon (to the ferryman): Have any deserters come through this way?

Ferryman: No, you are the first.

Prince Metternich, famed 19th century Austrian Foreign Minister, to the British Ambassador, Lord Dudley:

Metternich: You are the only Englishman who speaks good French. It is said that the common people in Vienna speak it better than the educated man in London.

Dudley: That may well be. Your Highness should recall that Napoleon has not been twice in London to teach them.

That depends, my Lord, whether I embrace your mistress or your principles.

Attributed to JOHN WILKES (1727–97), responding to Lord Sandwich who had told Wilkes that he would die either of the pox or on the gallows

The atrocious crime of being a young man, which the honourable gentleman has with such spirit and decency charged upon me, I shall attempt neither to palliate nor to deny, but content myself

with wishing that I shall be one of those whose follies shall cease with their youth, and not of that number who are ignorant in spite of experience.

WILLIAM PITT (the Elder), answering the criticism of Robert Walpole, 1741

Yes, I am a Jew, and when the ancestors of the right honourable gentleman were brutal savages in an unknown land, mine were priests in the temple of Solomon.

BENJAMIN DISRAELI, replying to Daniel O'Connell, Irish Catholic leader, who had ridiculed his Jewish ancestry, House of Commons, 1835

Mr Speaker, I withdraw. Half the Cabinet are not asses.

DISRAELI was once upbraided by the Speaker and asked to withdraw his assertion that 'Half the Cabinet are asses'

Student leader: We want to talk to you but we think it's impossible for you to understand us. You weren't raised in a time of instant communications or satellites and computers . . . we now live in an age of space travel . . . jet travel and high speed electronics. You didn't have those things when you were young. Ronald Reagan: No, we didn't have those things when we were your age – we invented them.

RONALD REAGAN, when Governor of California, responding to a group of student demonstrators who had occupied his office

They've got a point. I don't have any experience in running up a $4,000 billion debt.

ROSS PEROT, responding to George W. Bush who had accused him of having no experience in government, US presidential campaign, 1992

And when we open our dykes, the waters are ten feet deep.

QUEEN WILHELMINA OF THE NETHERLANDS responding to the threatening boast of Kaiser Wilhelm II of Germany shortly before the First World War that 'all my guardsmen are seven feet tall' (attrib.)

Fourteen? The good Lord only has ten.

GEORGES CLEMENCEAU, French Prime Minister, responding to US President Woodrow Wilson's announcement to Congress of his Fourteen Points peace plan of January 1918 to end the First World War

Yes, a relief – like crapping in your pants.

ALEXIS LEGER, French aide at the 1938 Munich conference which sacrificed Czechoslovakia to Hitler, in response to his colleague Paul Stehlin's declaration that 'this agreement is a relief'

At a state banquet during a visit to Brazil, Prince Philip was introduced to a Brazilian general whose uniform was resplendent with medals and who, when Philip enquired, said they had been won in the war.

Prince Philip: I didn't know Brazil was in the war that long.

The general: At least, sir, I didn't get them for marrying my wife.

Viscount Kilmuir: A cook would have been given more notice of his dismissal.

Harold Macmillan: Ah, but good cooks are hard to find.

Prime Minister's riposte to his aggrieved former Lord Chancellor, one of the seven victims of Macmillan's 'night of the long knives' Cabinet reshuffle, July 1962. Kilmuir had been continuously in office for eleven years

I shall not dance with you for three reasons. First, because you are drunk. Second, because this is not a waltz but the Peruvian national anthem. And third, because I am not a beautiful lady in red; I am the cardinal bishop of Lima.

Legendary attributed response at a diplomatic reception to the drunken behaviour of GEORGE BROWN, Labour Foreign Secretary 1966–8

Because I'm married to the Queen of Denmark.

Response to LORD JANNER who enquired of a fellow guest at a cocktail party why he chose to live in Denmark, August 1999

Well, I hope your f**king feathers all fall out.

GEORGE BROWN, to Len Williams, Labour Party general secretary who had just been appointed Governor-General of Mauritius by Harold Wilson, 1968. Brown, who disliked Williams, had asked whether his new position required him 'to wear one of those plumed hats.' Williams had replied that it did

If it's a boy, it will be named after our late King George. If it's a girl, it will be Elizabeth, after our Queen. If, however, it is merely wind, as I suspect, it will be named John Foster Dulles.

WINSTON CHURCHILL, responding to Dulles, American Secretary of State 1953–9 who had patted his growing stomach and asked, 'When's it due, Winston?' (attrib.)

To make sure the f**ker was planted.

CHARLES HAUGHEY, on the only reason he attended the funeral of political rival Erskine Childers, November 1974

It's a pity others had to leave theirs on the ground at Goose Green to prove it.

NEIL KINNOCK, replying during a TV election debate, to a member of the audience who had shouted that Margaret Thatcher 'had guts', 1983. Mr Kinnock points out that there were demands that he withdraw his statement. He didn't, he says, 'not least because several people in, or associated with, the Forces took the trouble to let me know that they thought I should stand by what I said'

Very well. Good day.

CLEMENT ATTLEE'S response to a young MP, to whom he had offered a post in his government, who had expressed humbleness about his abilities to do the job

I will never allow a Royal Dockyard to be closed. And why do I say this?
(Voice from hall) Because you're in Chatham . . .

HAROLD WILSON at a 1960s campaign rally

223

He was the father of a President of the United States.

HARRY TRUMAN, responding to stories that his father had been a failure

Dewey: I'm glad to see so many children in the crowd. You should be grateful because I got you a day off school.
Child: Today is Saturday!

THOMAS DEWEY, US Republican candidate, presidential campaign, 1948

John F. Kennedy talking to a businessman, trying to counter a prevailing mood of pessimism in the business world in 1961:
Things look great. Why, if I wasn't President, I'd be buying stock myself.
Businessman: If you weren't President, so would I.

In your heart, you know he's right.

ELECTION SLOGAN OF REPUBLICAN CANDIDATE BARRY GOLDWATER, presidential campaign, 1964

In your guts, you know he's nuts.

DEMOCRATIC PARTY RESPONSE, 1964

US Senator Bill Bradley, at an official dinner during the 2000 election, being refused two pats of butter by the waiter:
Bradley: Do you know who I am? I'm a member of the US Senate. I'm chairman of the Appropriations Committee. I'm a former basketball star. And I'm a candidate for the US Presidency.
Waiter: Do you know who I am? I'm the guy in charge of the butter.

It's like a vasectomy – you can have all of the fun without any of the responsibility.

STEVEN NORRIS, former Transport minister, on the benefits of a peerage

Ouch! Sitting Ducks

Prime Minister Stanley Baldwin was sitting in a railway compartment with one other traveller, who stared at him intently before he leaned over and tapped his knee:

Man: You're Baldwin, aren't you? You were at Harrow in '84.

Baldwin: Yes, you're right.

Man (after a long pause): Tell me, what are you doing now?

Quoted by Roy Jenkins, *Baldwin*, 1987

Roy Jenkins's travels in search of a seat after forming the SDP took the new party leader to Glasgow Hillhead in March 1982. Canvassing in the by-election, he approached a man of Indian extraction, asking:

Jenkins: How long have you been here?

Man: A lot longer than you.

I'm sorry Mr Jenkins, we only have Benson and Hedges.

Story told by former Labour leader NEIL KINNOCK of Roy Jenkins, a noted gastronomic bon viveur, visiting a tiny Welsh village restaurant and asking the waitress for asparagus tips.

When Uncle Jack was your age, he was President of the United States.

Schoolboy, to 1972 Democratic vice-presidential candidate Sargent Shriver, a Kennedy in-law, who tried to inspire the class to work harder by telling them that Abraham Lincoln at their age had walked twelve miles back and forth to school every day

After each of my foreign trips, I have made recommendations which were adopted.

RICHARD NIXON, Republican presidential candidate, who had been Eisenhower's Vice-President for eight years, attempting to stress his experience over opponent John F. Kennedy, campaign, 1960

If you give me a week, I might think of one.

President EISENHOWER, to reporters who asked what these had been, 1960

225

Ouch! Sitting Ducks

Representative Anne Mueller: Mr Speaker, will you please turn me on.

House Speaker, Tom Murphy: Thirty years ago, I would have tried.

Exchange in the Georgia state assembly. Mueller complained that her microphone was switched off

Like many car accidents, they are a matter of perception.

BOB PACKWOOD, US senator for Oregon, accounting for twenty-nine accusations of sexual harassment against him, TV interview, March 1994

Forgive me, Senator, but when you have twenty-nine car crashes, there's something wrong with the way you're driving.

BARBARA WALTERS, the interviewer, March 1994

American workers should draw a mushroom cloud and put underneath it: 'Made in America by lazy and illiterate Americans and tested in Japan.'

ERNEST HOLLINGS, US senator for South Carolina, responding to remarks by Yoshio Sakurauchi, speaker of the Japanese Parliament, who attacked the American workforce as lazy and illiterate, 1992

Princess Diana, during a walkabout in South Australia in 1983, tousled the hair of a little boy in the crowd.

Princess: Why aren't you at school today?

The boy: I was sent home because I've got head lice.

We've got a corporal at the top, not a cavalry officer.

FRANCIS PYM, Foreign Secretary, on Margaret Thatcher, 1982. The remark, made privately, reached her ears, enraging her. It may have helped seal his fate

Landslides, on the whole, don't produce successful governments.

PYM, general election campaign, 1983. This did seal his fate

Ouch! Sitting Ducks

There is an ex-chief Whips' club. They are very unusual people.

MARGARET THATCHER'S response, the following day. Pym was returned to the back benches immediately after the election

During a filibuster on the Antarctic Minerals Bill, July 1989:
Mr Hardy (Wentworth, Lab): I asked Lech Walesa . . . Lech Walesa does not speak English, but he stuck his thumb up and gave me a broad grin . . .
The Deputy Speaker: Order. I think that the Hon. Gentleman is on the wrong Pole.

Graham Allen (Nottingham North, Lab): To ask the Lord President of the Council, how many parliamentary questions have been answered in the past twelve months with the statement that the required figures are not available.
Tony Newton: This information is not in a readily available form and could only be provided at disproportionate cost.

HANSARD, November 1993

Dennis Skinner (Bolsover, Lab): To ask the Minister for the Civil Service, how many civil servants in employment at the latest date are (a) men or (b) women.
Tim Renton: All of them.

HANSARD, February 1992

George Galloway: Why do people take such an instant dislike to me?
A colleague: Because it saves time.

Reported exchange, 1992

If you select me, I shall certainly join.

MICHAEL MATES, asked about his record in the Tory Party, Hampshire East selection meeting

Jack Straw, Home Secretary visiting a Bournemouth old peoples' home during the 1999 Labour Party Conference, to a resident: Do you know who I am?
Resident: No dear, but if you ask matron, she will tell you

Charles Kennedy, visiting a Bournemouth hospital in September 2000, greeted by a patient who exclaimed 'I voted for you at the election.': Great. What are you in here for?
Patient: Brain surgery.

David Cameron, on the campaign trail, 2001, being told that an elderly woman he was trying to canvass could not stop to talk because she had just lost her dog: Can I help look for it?
Woman: No, it just died.

Rejoice! Rejoice!

MARGARET THATCHER, after the recapture of South Georgia during the Falklands War, 1982

Rejoice! Rejoice!

SIR EDWARD HEATH, after Margaret Thatcher's defeat in the Conservative leadership contest, 1990

They're from my husband's funeral.

Response to an MP, whose identity was not disclosed, canvassing in the Kincardine and Deeside by-election, who had 'offered fulsome congratulations on the stunning floral display in the constituent's hallway', *The Times* report, 1991

John Prescott: I've already rung up my mother to give her my Mother's Day greeting. Have you?
David Frost, whose mother had died 11 years before: No. My dear mother is out of range, as it were.

228

John Prescott, after a convoluted monologue in a BBC interview with Nick Robinson, March 2000 : Can I do that again? That was crap.
Nick Robinson: You're live

11

Aha!

Transparent Euphemisms

Public life can infect its denizens with a pathological inability to spit it out. Who did these people think they were kidding? . . .

I do not like this word 'bomb'. It is not a bomb. It is a device which is exploding.

JACQUES LE BLANC, French ambassador to New Zealand, responding to criticism of France's nuclear tests in the Pacific, October 1995

The war situation has developed, not necessarily to Japan's advantage.

EMPEROR HIROHITO announcing the Japanese surrender after the dropping of the two atomic bombs, national broadcast, 1945

[Nuclear war is] something that may not be desirable.

ED MEESE, counsellor in the Reagan White House, 1982

This is not war. The marines are not in combat.

WHITE HOUSE response to Congressional attempts to vote to withdraw US troops from Beirut after the first fatalities in the peacekeeping force in August 1983. Under the War Powers Act, Congress could invoke its rights only in war conditions

The crucial point is that they are in a stationary position.

Further WHITE HOUSE elaboration when Congressional leaders asserted that war conditions did exist since American troops were returning fire, 1983

Nothing has changed. We are not leaving Lebanon. The marines are being deployed two or three miles to the west.

CASPAR WEINBERGER, US Defense Secretary, denying in 1984 that the movement of US troops amounted to a retreat. The deployment 'two or three miles to the west' just happened to be from land bases on Lebanese soil to ships offshore

This is a strengthened peace implementation force.

GEORGE ROBERTSON, Defence Secretary announcing the reinforcement of British troops in Kosovo, May 1999

We are not at war with Egypt. We are in armed conflict.

SIR ANTHONY EDEN, Prime Minister, after the Anglo-French landings in Suez, 1956

We were not micro-managing Grenada intelligence-wise until about that time frame.

US Admiral WESLEY MCDONALD, explaining why America was taken by surprise by the coup on Grenada in 1983, which prompted the US airborne invasion (which was officially termed not an invasion but 'a *pre-dawn vertical insertion*')

We have no political prisoners, only communists and others involved in conspiracies against the country.

PRESIDENT PARK CHUNG-LEE of South Korea, 1974

It's not that it was removed. The example did not persist.

DEPARTMENT OF HEALTH CIVIL SERVANT, explaining why a government policy document on the NHS had been redrafted to omit a reference to a black family, 1997

[It is just] a significant change in direction away from meeting the objective.

Explanatory note in the Quality of Life Barometer produced by the DEPARTMENT FOR ENVIRONMENT, FOOD AND RURAL AFFAIRS regarding any target that was failing to be met, March 2002

Aha! Transparent Euphemisms

I would not say there was an argument. There was a discussion and some different views.

IAN PETERS, deputy director-general, British Chambers of Commerce, on a row over the organisation's poll on whether Britain should join the single European currency, November 1999

Two wongs don't make a white.

ARTHUR CALDWELL, Australian immigration minister on the 'White Australia Policy', 1947

'Burnham Category II/III courses may or may not be advanced and poolable. A Burnham Category II/III course which is not poolable is not poolable only because it is not advanced, i.e. it does not require course approval as an advanced course. It is therefore wrong to ascribe it as a non-poolable advanced (non-designated) course. Non-poolable courses are non-advanced by definition. I think that the problem you have described probably results from confusion here.'

'Explanatory' letter from the Department of Education and Science, quoted by LORD ELWYN JONES, House of Lords, 1987

The slowing in the universities' rate of expansion experienced in the 1970s was replaced in the early 1980s by an expenditure-led policy of contraction.

GOVERNMENT REPORT ON UNIVERSITY FUNDING, *Review of the University Grants Commission*, chaired by Lord Croham, deploying an elegant euphemism for spending cuts, February 1987

We are satisfied . . . that this experience seriously compromises the welfare of the fox.

LORD BURNS, conclusion of his independent committee's enquiry into fox hunting, June 2000

Aha! Transparent Euphemisms

I did not desire to fire Mr Fitzgerald. I prefer to use the correct term, which is to abolish his job.

ROBERT SEAMONS, US Secretary for the Air Force, dismissing Ernest Fitzgerald, an efficiency expert who had identified massive overspending, 1969

A wage-based premium.

PRESIDENT CLINTON, pledged not to raise taxes, announcing the means (taxation) by which his health care plan would be financed, 1993

User fee.

PRESIDENT REAGAN'S ADMINISTRATION, also pledged not to raise taxes, describing the four cents a gallon increase in the federal petrol tax, 1983

Food-insecure.

Description of the world's hungry population, used at the WORLD FOOD SUMMIT, Rome, November 1996

Very low food security.

US DEPARTMENT OF AGRICULTURE Annual Report, November 2006 replacement for 'hungry' to define the experience of 4.4 million Americans; a USDA sociologist said hunger is not a scientifically quantifiable term

A very large, potentially disruptive re-entry system.

PENTAGON description of the Titan II nuclear missile, 600 times more powerful than the Hiroshima bomb, 1980s

[The test] was terminated five minutes earlier than planned [after the missile] impacted the ground prematurely.

US Air Force explanation of a cruise missile crash, 1986

Rapid oxidation; energetic disassembly; abnormal evolution.

Terminology introduced by the US nuclear power industry after the 1979 Three Mile Island accident for official reporting of incidents. The terms were to be used instead of 'fire', 'explosion' and 'accident'

Like Grandma's nightshirt – it covered everything.

US President LYNDON JOHNSON on the notorious Tonkin Gulf Resolution passed by Congress in August 1964 authorising military action in Vietnam. It followed attacks by Vietnamese naval vessels on US patrol boats in the Gulf of Tonkin, some of which are now regarded as having been fabricated by US intelligence who were desperate to show Congressional leaders there were grounds for stepping up action against the Communist North. The resolution was the only legal basis ever used for America's war in Vietnam

[The suspect was] eliminate[d] with extreme prejudice.

CIA description of its execution of a suspected double agent in Vietnam, 1971

This is the operative statement. The others are inoperative.

RONALD ZIEGLER, Nixon press secretary, after the President had admitted the involvement of senior White House aides in the Watergate cover-up, reminded by reporters of previous statements denying involvement, April 1973

The ministry cancels this portion of the minister's remarks as non-existent.

SOUTH KOREAN DEFENCE MINISTRY statement sanitizing Lee Jong-Koo's remarks when he publicly advocated military raids on North Korean nuclear facilities, April 1991

An incomplete success.

PRESIDENT JIMMY CARTER describing the failed attempt to rescue the US embassy hostages held in Iran, 1980

It is a tricky problem to find the particular calibration in timing that would be appropriate to stem the acceleration in risk premiums created by falling incomes without prematurely aborting the decline in the inflation-generated risk premiums.

ALAN GREENSPAN, chairman of the President's Council of Economic Advisers, testifying to a Senate committee why the Nixon administration's anti-inflation policies weren't working, 1974

Aha! Transparent Euphemisms

I guess I should warn you, if I turn out to be particularly clear, you've probably misunderstood what I've said.

GREENSPAN, then chairman of the Federal Reserve Board, speech to the Economic Club, 1988

To the extent that when one measures real interest rates by effectively subtracting the inflation rate from nominal interest rates, if there is a bias in the inflation rate, and it hasn't changed very significantly, it means that the level of inflation that – once it subtracts from the nominal interest rate – is lower across the board of history, and that the real interest rate measured is correspondingly higher.

GREENSPAN, June 1994

We have no political prisoners. We have political internal exiles.

Chilean President AUGUSTO PINOCHET, 1975

We have not closed down our parties, just suspended their activities.

General KENAN EVREN, military ruler of Turkey, April 1981, six months after he seized power in a coup

It became necessary to destroy the village in order to save it.

US ARMY REPORT on the razing of Ben Tre, South Vietnam, 1968

It was not a bombing of Cambodia. It was a bombing of North Vietnamese in Cambodia.

HENRY KISSINGER, 1973

You always write it's bombing, bombing, bombing. It's not bombing, it's air support.

COLONEL DAVID OPFER, US Air Force attaché at the American embassy in Cambodia, to journalists, 1974

We are conducting limited duration protective reaction air strikes.

US ARMY SPOKESMAN, Vietnam, describing a bombing campaign

Unlawful or arbitrary deprivation of life.

Phrase adopted by the US STATE DEPARTMENT for 'killing' in its 1984-85 annual global human rights review. A spokesman said, 'We found the term "killing" too broad'

[I] was provided with additional input that was radically different from the truth. I assisted in furthering that version.

Lt Col OLIVER NORTH, refusing to admit he lied during the Iran-Contra scandal, July 1990

You won the election; but I won the count.

ANASTASIO SOMOZA, dictator of Nicaragua, 1967–79, to his defeated opponent in the fixed presidential election which ushered in his regime. His family dynasty had ruled the country since 1937

I didn't accept it. I received it.

RICHARD ALLEN, national security adviser to President Reagan, explaining how he came to gain $1,000 and two watches from journalists in return for an exclusive interview with Mrs Reagan

I did not kick the minister. I drove her away with the point of my shoe.

ALESSANDRA MUSSOLINI, Italian member of parliament and granddaughter of the fascist dictator, on a confrontation during a television discussion show with Katia Bellillo, the Minister for Equal Opportunities, known for her enthusiasm for kick-boxing, February 2001

Outside of the killings, we have one of the lowest crime rates.

MARION BARRY, Mayor of Washington DC, the city with the highest murder rate in America, 1989

I haven't committed a crime. What I did was fail to comply with the law.

DAVID DINKINS, Mayor of New York, fending off accusations of tax evasion

It should be made quite clear that pharmacists are not striking for more money but for an improved rate of pay for their profession.

MICHAEL BEAMAN, Guild of Hospital Pharmacists Council, 1982

It was not a defeat. I was merely placed third in the polls.

BILL PITT, first successful Liberal/SDP Alliance candidate, after winning the Croydon NW by-election in 1981, on his previous attempt to win the seat at the 1979 general election. (How he described his non-defeat in 1983, when he finished second to the Conservative, is not recorded.)

I am pro-choice with limitations, pro-life with exceptions.

JOHN WARNER, Virginia Senator since 1979, campaign statement on abortion

Yes I can get angry . . . But if you look at the decisions I make, they are all pretty rational ones. I don't pursue vendettas or punch people on the nose.

JOHN PRESCOTT, Deputy Labour Leader, *Guardian* interview 1994

Our legal advice is that Mr Prescott was defending himself.

LABOUR PARTY spokesman after John Prescott, Deputy Prime Minister, punched a bystander who threw an egg at him during an election visit to Rhyl, 16 May 2001. It turned out to be the highlight of the dullest campaign in living memory

12

Ira . . . aaagh

– Confounded Facts

The US-led invasion of Iraq in 2003 unleashed the most divisive war-related controversy in British politics since Suez nearly half a century before. The decision by Tony Blair's government to unequivocally back America in its post-9/11 pursuit of Arab extremism polarised the country. Certain, after more than a decade of playing cat-and-mouse with Saddam Hussein, that Iraq possessed a hidden stockpile of weapons of mass destruction – nuclear, biological and chemical – the Bush-Blair case for ousting the Iraqi dictator seemed self-evident.

Arguably, it all started way back in 1990 . . .

We don't have much to say about your Arab–Arab border differences such as you have with Kuwait. All we hope is that you solve this quickly.

US Ambassador APRIL GLASPIE, fateful conversation with Iraqi leader Saddam Hussein, shortly before his invasion of Kuwait, July 1990. The comments were widely regarded within Iraq as the US indicating it would not act if Iraq seized Kuwait

The 1991 Gulf campaign defeated, but did not displace, Saddam. For the next 12 years, UN weapons' inspections tortuously tried to establish whether Iraq's arsenal had been disposed of. 9/11 brought the issue back to the top of America's worry list.

Ira . . . aaagh – Confounded Facts

Iraq continues to flaunt its hostility toward America and to support terror. The Iraqi regime has plotted to develop anthrax, and nerve gas, and nuclear weapons for over a decade . . . This is a regime that has something to hide from the civilized world.

President GEORGE W. BUSH, State of the Union speech, January 2002

Simply stated, there is no doubt that Saddam Hussein now has weapons of mass destruction [and] there is no doubt that he is amassing them to use against our friends, against our allies and against us.

Vice-President DICK CHENEY, speech Nashville, Tennessee, 26 August 2002

The President of the United States and the Secretary of Defense would not assert as plainly and bluntly as they have that Iraq has weapons of mass destruction if it was not true, and if they did not have a solid basis for saying it.

ARI FLEISCHER, White House spokesman, December 2002

Well, there is no question that we have evidence and information that Iraq has weapons of mass destruction, biological and chemical particularly . . . all this will be made clear in the course of the operation, for whatever duration it takes.

ARI FLEISCHER, the day after war started, March 2003

The British government has learned that Saddam Hussein recently sought significant quantities of uranium from Africa.

President GEORGE W. BUSH, State of the Union address, January 2003. The claim, which later turned out to be unfounded, had been deleted from a speech Bush had made three months earlier because the CIA doubted its truth. It found its way back in because George Tenet, the CIA Director, had not reviewed the draft and the White House speechwriters had forgotten the earlier CIA warning

Ira . . . aaagh – Confounded Facts

It [the intelligence service] concludes that Iraq has chemical and biological weapons, that Saddam has continued to produce them, that he has existing and active military plans for the use of chemical and biological weapons, which could be activated within 45 minutes, including against his own Shia population; and that he is actively trying to acquire nuclear weapons capability.

TONY BLAIR, House of Commons, September 2002

It's a slam-dunk case.

GEORGE TENET, CIA Director, replying to President Bush's concerns about the quality of the intelligence on Iraq's weapons of mass destruction, December 2002, publicly revealed for the first time in April 2004 by Bob Woodward's book, *Plan of Attack*

The intelligence is clear: Saddam continues to believe his WMD programme is essential both for internal repression and for external aggression . . . The biological agents we believe Iraq can produce include anthrax, botulinum toxin, aflatoxin and ricin. All eventually result in excruciatingly painful death.

TONY BLAIR, House of Commons, February 2003

The facts and Iraq's behavior show that Saddam Hussein and his regime are concealing their efforts to produce more weapons of mass destruction.

COLIN POWELL, Secretary of State, laying out the US intelligence case to the UN Security Council, February 2003

My colleagues, every statement I make today is backed up by sources, solid sources. These are not assertions. What we're giving you are facts and conclusions based on solid intelligence.

POWELL

The Iraqis have never accounted for all of the biological weapons they admitted they had and we know they had . . . This is evidence, not conjecture. This is true. This is all well-documented . . .

POWELL

Ira . . . aaagh – Confounded Facts

There can be no doubt that Saddam Hussein has biological weapons and the capability to rapidly produce more, many more. And he has the ability to dispense these lethal poisons and diseases in ways that can cause massive death and destruction.

POWELL

We know that Saddam Hussein is determined to keep his weapons of mass destruction; he's determined to make more.

POWELL

We are asked now seriously to accept that in the last few years – contrary to all history, contrary to all intelligence – Saddam decided unilaterally to destroy those weapons. I say that such a claim is palpably absurd.

TONY BLAIR, House of Commons, March 2003

In contrast to the threat, the effort required to sort it out was negligible.

The idea that it's going to be a long, long, long battle of some kind I think is belied by the fact of what happened in 1990 . . . Five days or five weeks or five months, but it certainly isn't going to last any longer than that.

DONALD RUMSFELD, US Secretary of Defense, November 2002

I promise you it will be swift and decisive.

BUSH on the plans for regime change in Iraq, September 2002

I can't tell you exactly how many days or how many weeks. But by historical standards, this will be a short war.

RICHARD PERLE, Chairman of the US Defense Policy Board, March 2003

Ira . . . aaagh – Confounded Facts

My own judgment based on my time as Secretary of Defense, and having operated in this area in the past, I'm confident that our troops will be successful, and I think it'll go relatively quickly . . . weeks rather than months.

DICK CHENEY, Vice-President, March 2003, shortly before the invasion. By the beginning of October 2008, it was 289 weeks and counting

We have said all along that this will be a tough fight.

Maj-Gen KEVIN BERGNER, military spokesman, May 2008, after a series of attacks on US forces in Iraq that made April 2008 the bloodiest month for American forces since the previous September

Cheney had been Defense Secretary during the first Gulf War in 1991. Then, he appeared to have drawn very different lessons.

The question in my mind is how many additional American casualties is Saddam worth? And the answer is not very damned many. So I think we got it right . . . we were not going to go get bogged down in the problems of trying to take over and govern Iraq.

CHENEY, as Defense Secretary, August 1992, explaining the decision not to invade Iraq after the liberation of Kuwait.

All of a sudden you've got a battle you're fighting in a major built-up city, a lot of civilians are around, significant limitations on our ability to use our most effective technologies and techniques . . . Once we had rounded him up and gotten rid of his government, then the question is what do you put in his place? You know, you then have accepted the responsibility for governing Iraq.

CHENEY, August 1992. As Vice-President he was one of the strongest advocates for the invasion

What kind of government are you going to establish? Is it going to be a Kurdish government, or a Shia government, or a Sunni government . . . or some mixture? You will have, I think by that time, lost the support of the Arab coalition that was so crucial to our operations over there . . . I would guess if we had gone in there, I would still have forces in Baghdad today, we'd be running the country. We would not have been able to get everybody out and bring everybody home.

CHENEY, presciently, August 1992

Iraq was invaded in March 2003. On the eve, one British Cabinet Minister took an apparently clear stance:

Absolutely. There's no question about that. If there is not UN authority for military action or if there is not UN authority for the reconstruction of the country, I will not uphold a breach of international law or this undermining of the UN and I will resign from the government . . . I think it's time for cards on the table. People are speculating and making all sorts of statements about my intentions. I think I owe it to my colleagues in the government and members of the Labour party to just be truthful about my position.

CLARE SHORT, International Development Secretary, 9 March 2003, asked whether she would resign if there was no mandate from the United Nations for war

But on the other hand . . .

I think I could add a bit if I stayed, but it's a very, very, very good department and you can't stay and defend the indefensible in order to do some other things that you think need doing. I can rely on others I think to do what is right to rebuild Iraq.

CLARE SHORT, same interview, asked whether she would have less influence in the reconstruction of Iraq if she left

So when it came to the crunch . . .

I have now decided that [leaving the Government] would be cowardly, because I would be offering no alternative way forward or making any contribution to resolving the problems ahead of us.

CLARE SHORT, 18 March, after the start of the war, without a UN mandate, rescinding her resignation. She eventually resigned two months later

243

Back in the weapons hunt . . .

It is not like a treasure hunt, where you just run around looking everywhere hoping you find something.

DONALD RUMSFELD, US Secretary of Defense, on the search for chemical and biological weapons in Iraq, April 2003

As I have said throughout, I have no doubt that they will find the clearest possible evidence of Saddam's weapons of mass destruction.

TONY BLAIR, House of Commons, June 2003

There is no reliable information on whether Iraq is producing and stockpiling chemical weapons.

US DEFENSE INTELLIGENCE AGENCY, in a report dated September 2002, leaked in June 2003, which seemed to contradict the Administration's case for disarming Iraq

[The report] is not in any way intended to portray the fact that we had any doubts that such a program existed.

Vice-Admiral LOWELL JACOBY, US Defense Intelligence Agency director, after the report was made public, June 2003

Going into the war against Iraq, we had very strong intelligence. I've been in this business for 20 years. And some of the strongest intelligence cases that I've seen, key judgments by our intelligence community that Saddam Hussein . . . had biological and chemical weapons . . .

CONDOLEEZZA RICE, US National Security Adviser, July 2003

I don't concede it at all that the intelligence at the time was wrong . . . I have absolutely no doubt at all that we will find evidence of weapons of mass destruction programmes.

TONY BLAIR, to Commons Liaison Committee, July 2003

Ira . . . aaagh – Confounded Facts

The Iraqis had over two decades to develop these weapons. And hiding them was an essential part of their program.

DAVID KAY, overseer of the hunt for weapons of mass destruction in Iraq, August 2003, after testifying before the US Senate Armed Services Committee

We've found a couple of semi-trailers . . . I would deem that conclusive evidence, if you will, that he did have programs for weapons of mass destruction.

DICK CHENEY, US Vice President, asserting that Saddam Hussein had been developing illegal weapons, January 2004

I have not seen [a] smoking gun, concrete evidence about the connection, but I think the possibility of such connections did exist, and it was prudent to consider them at the time.

COLIN POWELL, US Secretary of State, in response to continued doubts about links between Saddam Hussein and al-Qaeda, one of the reasons the Bush Administration cited for going to war, January 2004

I don't think they existed . . . I don't think there was a large-scale production program in the '90s.

DAVID KAY, stepping down as leader of the US hunt for weapons of mass destruction in Iraq, saying his work was finished, January 2004

It is unlikely that Iraq could have destroyed, hidden or sent out of the country the hundreds of tons of chemical and biological weapons . . . that officials claimed were present without the United States detecting some sign of this activity.

CARNEGIE ENDOWMENT FOR INTERNATIONAL PEACE, in a report alleging that the Bush Administration misrepresented the threat from illicit weapons in Iraq, January 2004

Back at No 10 . . .

I don't think it's surprising we will have to look for them. I'm confident that when the Iraq Survey Group has done its work we will find what's happened to those weapons because he had them.

TONY BLAIR, interview BBC Arabic Service, December 2003

Ira . . . aaagh – Confounded Facts

I have absolutely no doubt in my mind that the intelligence was genuine.

BLAIR, *Observer*, January 2004

We were almost all wrong, and I certainly include myself.

DAVID KAY, ex-Head of the Iraq Survey Group, sent into Iraq to search for weapons of mass destruction, to US Senate Armed Service Committee, January 2004, shortly after he had resigned

What is true about David Kay's evidence, and this is something I have to accept, and is one of the reasons why I think we now need a new inquiry – it is true David Kay is saying we have not found large stockpiles of actual weapons.

BLAIR, to Common Liaison Committee, February 2004

I have to accept we haven't found them (WMD) and we may never find them, We don't know what has happened to them . . . They could have been removed. They could have been hidden. They could have been destroyed.

BLAIR, to Common Liaison Committee, July 2004

We expected, I expected to find actual usable, chemical or biological weapons after we entered Iraq . . . But I have to accept, as the months have passed, it seems increasingly clear that at the time of invasion, Saddam did not have stockpiles of chemical or biological weapons ready to deploy.

BLAIR, statement on Butler report, July 2004

I have to accept we haven't found them and we may not find them.

BLAIR, on the failure to locate any weapons of mass destruction, July 2004

The evidence about Saddam having actual biological and chemical weapons, as opposed to the capability to develop them, has turned out to be wrong. I acknowledge that and accept it. I simply point out, such evidence was agreed by the whole international community, not least because Saddam had used such weapons against his own people and neighbouring countries.

BLAIR, Labour Party conference, September 2004

President Bush controversially signaled the supposed end of combat operations in May, but the war annoyingly kept going, as did the backtracking . . .

Stuff happens. . . . Freedom's untidy, and free people are free to make mistakes and commit crimes and do bad things . . .

DONALD RUMSFELD, US Defense Secretary, Pentagon press conference, April 2003, on the looting of Iraqi government buildings following the capture of Baghdad

The MISSION ACCOMPLISHED sign, of course, was put up by the members of the USS *Abraham Lincoln*, saying that their mission was accomplished.

GEORGE W. BUSH, November 2003, on the banner that was used as a backdrop for his appearance aboard an aircraft carrier off the San Diego coast to declare the end of major combat operations in Iraq in May 2003. His spokesman later clarified: Though the Navy requested the banner, the White House made it. Five years later the White House finally conceded that Bush had 'paid a price' for the episode. Press Secretary Dana Perino attempted a retraction on 1 May 2008: 'President Bush is well aware that the banner should have been much more specific and said "Mission accomplished" for these sailors who are on this ship on their mission.' Her explanation failed, however, to reconcile this new interpretation of Bush's intentions with the President's own words on the occasion which declared the end of all major operations in the country

I actually did vote for the $87 billion before I voted against it.

US Presidential candidate JOHN KERRY, responding to Republican campaign ads that criticized his vote against a bill to authorise $87 billion in funds for postwar Iraq, March 2004

Confusion abounded . . .

I am way ahead of the commander in chief, and probably way ahead of my colleagues, and certainly of much of the country. But I believe this. I believe that he has used these weapons before, he has invaded another country, he views himself as a modern day Nebuchadnezzar . . . And I think we have to stand up to that.

Future Democratic Presidential candidate Senator JOHN KERRY, on the idea of going to war with Iraq, February 1998

Ira . . . aaagh – Confounded Facts

The President as I wrote . . . always reserves the right to act unilaterally to protect the interest of our country.

KERRY, September 2002

If Saddam Hussein is unwilling to bend to the international community's already existing order, then he will have invited enforcement, even if that enforcement is mostly at the hands of the United States, a right we retain even if the Security Council fails to act.

KERRY, writing in the *New York Times*, September 2002

I will be voting to give the President of the United States the authority to use force – if necessary – to disarm Saddam Hussein because I believe that a deadly arsenal of weapons of mass destruction in his hands is a real and grave threat to our security.

KERRY, October 2002

I think Saddam Hussein's weapons of mass destruction are a threat, and that's why I voted to hold him accountable and to make certain that we disarm him.

KERRY, National Public Radio interview, the day war started in Iraq, March 2003

George Bush has led and misled us on a course at odds with . . . our history. He has . . . lost the respect and the influence that we need to make our country safe. We are seeing the peril in Iraq every day . . . So long as Iraq remains an American intervention and not an international undertaking, we will face increasing danger and mounting casualties.

KERRY, September 2003

I believe the invasion of Iraq made us less secure and weaker in the war on terrorism.

KERRY, September 2004

Kerry seemed to have difficulty remembering what he really thought.

Yes, I would have voted for the authority [to go to war]. I believe it was the right authority for a president to have.

KERRY, asked in August 2004 during the presidential election campaign whether he would still have gone to war knowing Saddam Hussein did not possess weapons of mass destruction.

We should not have gone to war knowing the information that we know today. Knowing there was no imminent threat to America, knowing there were no weapons of mass destruction . . . I would not have gone to war.

KERRY, presidential campaign a month later, September 2004. His campaign team explained that the two views were not inconsistent. Voting to authorise war in Iraq, they maintained, was different from deciding to wage war.

Before resorting to his finest . . .

You bet we might have.

KERRY, asked if he would have gone to war against Saddam Hussein if he refused to disarm, US Presidential election 2004

But some weren't changing their minds

There are some who feel like the conditions are such that they can attack us. My answer is bring 'em on.

GEORGE W. BUSH, on Iraqi insurgents attacking US forces, July 2003

The President and I cannot prevent certain politicians from losing their memory or their backbone, but we're not going to sit by and let them rewrite history.

DICK CHENEY, US Vice President, November 2005, on Democrats accusing the Administration of misrepresenting prewar intelligence in Iraq, an allegation he called 'dishonest and reprehensible'

Ira . . . aaagh – Confounded Facts

Anyone with an ounce of sense would see it exactly opposite.

DONALD RUMSFELD, US Defense Secretary, January 2006, responding to reports, including one from the Pentagon, that the US military – ground forces in Iraq in particular – were overstretched

We don't start a job that we can't finish . . . That's the American way.

PAUL WOLFOWITZ, US Deputy Defense Secretary, September 2003, on the White House's request for $87 billion in military and reconstruction funds for Iraq and Afghanistan for the next year

When America gives a commitment, America will keep its commitment.

GEORGE W. BUSH to Iraqi Prime Minister Nouri al-Maliki assuring that the US will stand by Iraq's new government as it works to achieve stability, June 2006

There are neighbourhoods in Baghdad where you and I could walk through today.

Senator JOHN MCCAIN, candidate in the Presidential primaries, visit to a market in the Iraqi capital 1 April 2007, during which he was flanked by 22 soldiers, 10 armoured Humvees, and two Apache attack helicopters

Efforts at 'Iraqi-ization' of the war – getting Iraqi soldiers to fight the war – gathered pace in 2007. Watch this space . . .

Reflections . . . reality catching up

Those were the two dumbest words I ever said.

GEORGE TENET, former CIA director, May 2005, on his assurance to President Bush in 2002 that the CIA had 'slam dunk' evidence that Iraq had weapons of mass destruction

They never said there was an imminent threat. Rather, they painted an objective assessment . . . of a brutal dictator who was continuing his efforts to deceive and build programs that might constantly surprise us and threaten our interests.

TENET, CIA Director, defending his agency following criticism that it overstated the threat from weapons of mass destruction before the war in Iraq, February 2004

It's a blot. . . . [it] will always be a part of my record. It was painful. It's painful now.

COLIN POWELL, after his retirement as Secretary of State, on his infamous speech to the UN Security Council outlining the intelligence case against Iraq, September 2005

There were some people in the intelligence community who knew at that time that some of these sources were not good, and shouldn't be relied upon, and they didn't speak up. That devastated me.

POWELL, same interview

Why was there a banner that said 'Mission Accomplished' on the aircraft carrier? I have said a long time that reconstrution of Iraq would be a long, long, difficult process, but the conflict, the major conflict, is over, the regime change has been accomplished, and it's very appropriate.

Senator JOHN MCCAIN defending the 'Mission Accomplished' banner, interview *Fox News*, 11 June 2003

To state the obvious, I thought it was wrong at the time . . . those statements and comments did not comport with the facts on the ground.

MCCAIN, by now the Republican Presidential nominee, also to *Fox News*, 1 May 2008

In the lead-up to the Iraq war and its later conduct, I saw at a minimum, true dereliction, negligence and irresponsibility; at the worst, lying, incompetence and corruption . . .

Retired General ANTHONY ZINNI, former head of US Central Command, autobiography, June 2004

Ira . . . aaagh – Confounded Facts

What bothered me [was that] I was hearing a depiction of the intelligence that didn't fit what I knew. There was no solid proof, that I ever saw, that Saddam had WMD.

ZINNI, television interview, April 2006

Iraq remains the most significant near-term threat to US interests in the Arabian Gulf region. Despite claims that WMD efforts have ceased, Iraq probably is continuing clandestine nuclear research, retains stocks of chemical and biological munitions, and is concealing extended-range SCUD missiles, possibly equipped with [chemical-biological weapons] payloads.

ZINNI as Commander in Chief, Central Command, testifying to Congress, March 2000

Even if Baghdad reversed its course and surrendered all WMD capabilities, it retains the scientific, technical, and industrial infrastructure to replace agents and munitions within weeks or months.

ZINNI testimony, March 2000

One of the things I've learned is that sometimes words have consequences you don't intend them to. 'Bring 'em on' is a classic example.

GEORGE W. BUSH, January 2005, expressing regret for two statements he made during his first term. The other was his promise that the US would bring in Osama bin Laden 'dead or alive'

I learned some lessons about expressing myself maybe in a little more sophisticated manner.

BUSH, at press conference with Prime Minister Tony Blair, when asked what missteps he most regrets over the course of the war in Iraq, May 2006. Bush said 'tough talk' – phrases like 'bring it on' – 'sent the wrong signal to people'

Anybody who is in a position to serve this country ought to understand the consequences of words.

BUSH, radio interview, November 2006

Ira . . . aaagh – Confounded Facts

I thought we would succeed quicker than we did, and I am disappointed by the pace of success.

BUSH, December 2006, at a press conference with British Prime Minister Tony Blair, answering a question about whether he would acknowledge his failures and change course

It's bad in Iraq. Does that help?

BUSH, after being asked by a reporter whether he was in denial about Iraq, December 2006

So?

US Vice-President DICK CHENEY, March 2008, asked for his response to a poll showing that two-thirds of Americans did not believe the Iraq war was worth it

I'm gonna make a prediction. Write this down, Afghanistan and Iraq will lead that part of the world to democracy. They are going to be the catalyst to change the Middle East.

BUSH, to a meeting of Republican state governors, 20 September 2002, recounted in the memoirs of his press secretary, Scott McClellan, published May 2008

I think we are welcomed. But it was not a peaceful welcome.

BUSH, reflecting on the prediction that US troops in Iraq would be 'welcomed as liberators,' interview with *NBC News*, December 2005

Let the day-to-day judgements come and go. Be prepared to be judged by history.

Prime Minister TONY BLAIR, on the Iraq war

9/11, of course, started it all.

It's now a very good day to get out anything we want to bury.

JO MOORE, special adviser to Stephen Byers, Transport Secretary, in advice to senior management in the Transport Department an hour after the start of the terrorist attacks on the World Trade Center and the Pentagon, September 2001. It became public knowledge a month later

This crusade, this war on terrorism, is going to take a while.

GEORGE W. BUSH, 16 September 2001

Operation Infinite Justice.

Code name of the post-9/11 US war on global terrorism, dropped within a fortnight after concerns that it might deter Muslim nations from joining the coalition it is leading. Islamic scholars said that Muslims found the name deeply offensive because the Koran said that only Allah could grant infinite justice. The code name became Operation Enduring Freedom

Freedom Fries.

Label for French fries given in 2003 by the Republican-controlled US HOUSE OF REPRESENTATIVES canteen in response to French opposition to war in Iraq. The ban on 'French' lasted until August 2006. It also applied to French toast, which became Freedom Toast

There's an old poster out West, as I recall, that said, 'Wanted Dead Or Alive'. All I want and America wants is him brought to justice.

GEORGE W. BUSH, 17 September 2001

Let's give the terrorists a fair trial and then hang them.

US Senator GARY HART, post-9/11 perspective, 2001

But all in all, it's been a fabulous year for Laura and me.

GEORGE W. BUSH, summing up his first year in office, 20 December 2001

One thing we know for certain is that if Osama bin Laden is not in Afghanistan, he is either in another country or he is dead.

DONALD RUMSFELD, 2002

Ira . . . aaagh – Confounded Facts

Reports that say that something hasn't happened are always interesting to me, because as we know, there are known knowns; there are things we know we know. We also know there are known unknowns; that is to say we know there are some things we do not know. But there are also unknown unknowns – the ones we don't know we don't know.

RUMSFELD, US Secretary of Defense, press briefing, February 2002

It's not going to be a country club, but it's going to be humane.

DONALD RUMSFELD, 2002, on conditions at the Guantanamo Bay base where Al-Qaeda suspects were held after 9/11

They're very well treated down there. They're living in the tropics. They're well fed.

DICK CHENEY, US Vice President, defending the treatment of prisoners in Guantanamo Bay, Cuba, June 2005

They've never eaten better. They've never been treated better.

DUNCAN HUNTER, Republican Congressman from California, displaying a tray of lemon-baked fish and oven-fried chicken, which he said was reflective of the menu at Guantanamo Bay, June 2005

Guantanamo has become the gulag of our time.

IRENE KHAN, Secretary-General of Amnesty International, whose group issued a report castigating the US prison camp in Guantanamo Bay, May 2005

The murderous ideology of the Islamic radicals is the great challenge of our new century.

BUSH, speech on the 'war on terror', National Endowment for Democracy, Washington DC, October 2005

Now, in the 21st century, our nation is once again contending with an ideology that seeks to sow anger and hatred and despair – the ideology of Islamic extremism.

BUSH, speech, Colorado, May 2008

Ira . . . aaagh – Confounded Facts

God told me to strike at Al-Qaeda, and I struck them, and then He instructed me to strike at Saddam, which I did, and now I am determined to solve the problem in the Middle East.

BUSH, August 2003, oblivious to the irony.

God loves you and I love you and you can count on us both.

BUSH, speech, Philadelphia, December 2002

In the end, it was all too perplexing.

Why do they hate each other? Why do Sunnis kill Shiites? How do they tell the difference? They all look the same to me.

Republican Senator TRENT LOTT, on the Iraq insurgency, September 2006

13

Ugh!

– American Election Special

It's been called 'the great American shindig'. Every fourth year, Americans vote for a new Chief Executive. The trouble is, it takes them nearly two years to do it. In contrast to the British style of a snap call to the polls by the Prime Minister, a three week campaign and it's all over, the American nation indulges in a seemingly interminable elimination competition that starts almost as soon as the last inauguration is over. An American election is intensely personal. It is about voting for a personality first and foremost. The glare and scrutiny of the media is relentless. All this makes for a steady fount of material charting candidates' manoeuvrings while they try, as one individual politician, to appeal to the widest audience in perhaps the most diverse society on the planet . . . and also try to remember what they've said along the road for all those many, many months.

The 2008 campaign has been no exception . . .

[My great-grandparents] gave life to two renowned fighters, my great-uncle Wild Bill and my grandfather Sid McCain. ... Wild Bill joined the McCain name to an even more distinguished warrior family. His wife, Mary Louise Earle, was descended from royalty. She claimed as ancestors Scottish kings back to Robert the Bruce.

Senator JOHN McCAIN, Republican Party aspirant, whose campaign rested heavily on his credentials as a Vietnam war hero, claiming descent from Robert the Bruce in his 1999 memoir, *Faith of My Fathers.* The claim resurfaced during the campaign when McCain visited Britain in March 2008. Dr Kate Stevenson, mediaevalist at St Andrew's University, responded: 'what wonderful fiction ... any historian will tell you that it's virtually impossible to prove ancestry through the Middle Ages'. Another was a little kinder. Dr Bruce Durie of the University of Strathclyde commented that as Robert was thought to have had up to a dozen children, elementary mathematics suggested there could be as many as 200 million people distantly related to him. 'In that sense McCain probably is descended from Bruce. So am I. So are you. So is everyone.'

Hey, jerk.

McCain's standard election campaign greeting to visitors to his campaign bus, the Straight Talking Express, Presidential primaries, 2008

Bomb, bomb, bomb; bomb bomb Iran.

McCain, singing riposte (to the tune of the Beach Boys' *Barbara Ann*) on being asked about his post-Iraq policy towards Iran, Presidential campaign April 2007. When asked if he was not being insensitive, he replied, 'Insensitive to what? The Iranians?'

Make it a hundred. ...That would be fine with me.

McCain, to a questioner who asked if he supported President Bush's vision for keeping US troops in Iraq for 50 years

I'm not for, quote, privatizing Social Security. I never have been. I never will be.

McCain, Presidential nominee, June 2008

Without privatization, I don't see how you can possibly, over time, make sure that young Americans are able to receive Social Security benefits.

McCain, Senator, November 2004

I cannot in good conscience support a tax cut in which so many of the benefits go to the most fortunate among us, at the expense of middle class Americans who most need tax relief.

McCain, May 2001, breaking ranks with his party to oppose incoming President George Bush's programme of tax cuts, one of just two Republican senators to vote against them

I think it's very important that we make the Bush tax cuts permanent. I voted to make them permanent twice already . . . And if we don't make the tax cuts permanent, then they will experience what amounts to a tax increase.

McCain, candidates' debate, January 2008. He had earlier, in 2006, voted to extend the cuts when they were about to expire

Seizure World.

McCain, poking fun at the elderly of the Leisure World age bracket during his (successful)1986 Senate election campaign. He described the social grouping as one 'where 97 per cent vote and the other three per cent are in intensive care'. Twenty years later, campaigning to become the oldest elected President, he acknowledged that he was now one of them. 'I should have apologized immediately and fully for my discourtesy,' he said in January 2008

Don't tell me words don't matter. 'I have a dream.' Just words? 'We hold these truths to be self-evident, that all men are created equal.' Just words! 'We have nothing to fear but fear itself.' Just words – just speeches!

Democratic Party Presidential hopeful BARACK OBAMA, whose powers of rhetoric captured America's imagination in the 2008 campaign, getting caught out plagiarising from another candidate, February 2008. This eloquent passage was almost identical to one delivered by his friend Deval Patrick when winning election as Massachusetts governor in 2006, the first black to do so

[In] these small towns in Pennsylvania and . . . a lot of small towns in the Midwest [where] the jobs have been gone now for 25 years and nothing's replaced them, it's not surprising they get bitter, they cling to guns or religion . . . as a way to explain their frustrations.

OBAMA upsetting white voters in America's heartland during the Pennsylvania Presidential primary campaign, April 2008

Iran, Cuba, Venezuela — these countries are tiny compared to the Soviet Union. They don't pose a serious threat to us the way the Soviet Union posed a threat to us.

OBAMA, campaign rally, Oregon, 18 May 2008

Let me be absolutely clear: Iran is a grave threat.

OBAMA, campaign rally, Montana, 19 May 2008

I think it's time for us to end the embargo with Cuba. . . . [It] has failed to provide the sorts of rising standards of living and has squeezed the innocents in Cuba, and utterly failed in the effort to overthrow Castro . . . it's time for us to acknowledge that that particular policy has failed.

OBAMA, to a university audience, Illinois, January 2004

As president, I'll maintain the embargo – it's an important inducement for change.

OBAMA, to a Cuban-American audience, Miami, August 2007

If Obama was a white man, he would not be in this position. And if he was a woman of any colour, he would not be in this position. He happens to be very lucky to be who he is.

GERALDINE FERRARO, Clinton fundraiser and former Democratic vice-presidential candidate, uttering the sentiments that necessitated her resignation from Clinton's campaign two days later, March 2008

I helped to bring peace to Northern Ireland.

HILLARY CLINTON, Obama's Democratic Party rival, claiming a role in the 1998 Good Friday peace process, CNN interview, March 2008. Clinton claimed to have pulled together a meeting in Belfast City Hall 'bringing together for the first time Catholics and Protestants'. There is no record of such a meerting taking place. It later appeared that she was puffing up an appearance three years earlier in 1995 at a modest community gathering arranged by the American Consulate at the rather more mundane location of the Lamp Lighter Café in the Ormeau Road. Lord Trimble, the senior Unionist involved at the time, was less generous. 'I don't know there was much she did apart from accompanying Bill [Clinton] around.'

I remember landing under sniper fire. There was supposed to be some kind of a greeting ceremony at the airport, but instead we just ran with our heads down to get into the vehicles to get to our base.

CLINTON, campaigning in March 2008, describing her visit to Bosnia in 1996. In fact, television footage showed her and her daughter, Chelsea, calmly disembarking from the aircraft at Tuzla airport and being welcomed by a local girl. Clinton was shown hugging the child, wreathed in smiles for the cameras

I misspoke.

CLINTON explaining her account when confronted with the evidence of her rather more peaceful Bosnian reception. In the opinion of the *Sunday Times*, 'a classic Clintonism … You can say that you genuinely forgot, or got muddled up or fibbed. But Clinton cannot ever admit an actual mistake or a deliberate exaggeration. It was the same way in which Bill Clinton could never actually say that anything he did was ever "wrong". At most, it was always "inappropriate"'

I think, on balance, NAFTA has been good for New York and America.

CLINTON, when New York Senator, January 2004, on the North Amercian Free Trade Agreement introduced by husband Bill in 1994 linking the economies of the US, Canada and Mexico. Critics long claimed that its effect would be to encourage a transfer of jobs from the more expensive US economy to the other two, which in general it has. It became a topic of division amongst candidates in the Presidential primary campaign in 2008

I've long been a critic of the shortcomings of NAFTA.

CLINTON, Ohio primary, February 2008

I don't think it's useful to set a deadline because I think it sends a signal to the terrorists and the insurgents that they just have to wait us out.

CLINTON, interview with the Associated Press, February 2005

I am not one who feels comfortable setting exit strategies. We don't know what we're exiting from. We don't know what the situation is moving toward.

CLINTON, interview with CNN, May 2005

Ugh! – American Election Special

If you postpone a deadline that you set, you look weak. If you don't meet a deadline that you set, you look weak. You really give a lot of power to the people you don't want to empower.

CLINTON, interview with New York State's *Syracuse Post-Standard*, April 2006

I have a responsibility to look at this as carefully as I can and say what I believe, and what I believe is we're in a very dangerous situation and it doesn't lend itself to sound bites, and therefore I have resisted going along with ... my colleagues who feel passionately they need to call for a date ...

CLINTON, quoted in the *Washington Post*, May 2006

[I don't] think it is smart strategy to set a date certain. I do not agree that that is in the best interests ... of our country.

CLINTON, at a policy conference, Washington, June 2006. She was hissed and booed by the audience

Oh, yes, I'm on record as saying exactly that. As soon as I become president, we will start withdrawing within 60 days. We will move as carefully and responsibly as we can, one to two brigades a month, I believe, and we'll have nearly all the troops out by the end of the year, I hope.

CLINTON, January 2008, when asked during a candidates' debate in Las Vegas whether she would join with the declaration made by her rival Barack Obama that, if elected President, he would withdraw troops from Iraq within his first year

You know my husband did not wrap up the nomination in 1992 until he won the California primary somewhere in the middle of June, right? We all remember Bobby Kennedy was assassinated in June in California.

CLINTON, May 2008, resisting mounting pressure to concede the Democratic nomination to Obama. The comments to a newspaper in South Dakota, which was holding one of the final primaries, appeared to base her reluctance to give in on the fear (or, her critics suggested, hope) that Obama would be assassinated before the election. To add to the claims of insensitivity, the comments came only weeks after the commemoration of the 40th anniversary of the assassination of Martin Luther King. Clinton eventually conceded – but critics noted, by only suspended not terminating her campaign – in early June

I don't think you can criticize the president for trying to act on the belief that they have a substantial amount of chemical and biological stock . . . That is what I was always told.

Former President BILL CLINTON, speech in New York, April 2003

I supported the president when he asked for authority to stand up against weapons of mass destruction in Iraq.

CLINTON, speech in Mississippi, May 2003

I . . . opposed Iraq from the beginning

CLINTON, campaigning with wife Hillary in the Presidential primaries, November 2007

The best also-ran

I never said I was pro-choice, but my position was effectively pro-choice.

MITT ROMNEY, ex-Governor of Massachusetts and unsuccessful contender for the Republican presidential nomination in 2008, whose style became notorious for the mobility of his political positions as the campaign wore on

I believe that abortion should be safe and legal in this country . . . I believe that since Roe v. Wade has been the law for 20 years we should sustain and support it.

ROMNEY, campaigning for a Senate seat, October 1994

I respect and will protect a woman's right to choose.

ROMNEY, article in the *Boston Globe*, July 2005

I am pro-life. I believe that abortion is the wrong choice except in cases of incest, rape, and to save the life of the mother. I wish the people of America agreed, and that the laws of our nation could reflect that view. But while the nation remains so divided over abortion, I believe that the states, through the democratic process, should determine their own abortion laws and not have them dictated by judicial mandate.

ROMNEY, article in the same paper, three weeks later

Every piece of legislation which came to my desk [as] governor, I came down on the side of preserving the sanctity of life.

ROMNEY, during the presidential primary campaign, December 2007

There's a benefit to simplicity. I'm a strong believer in stating your position and not wavering,

ROMNEY, reported comments to a meeting of abortion activists, divulged to the *Los Angeles Times*, 2002

I saw my father march with Martin Luther King.

ROMNEY, whose father was Governor of Michigan in the mid-1960s at the time of the civil rights unrest in America. He made the claim several times during the presidential primaries in 2007, but investigative reporters established it was simply untrue. The Romney campaign claimed it was a reference to a visit King made to the small town of Grosse Point, Michigan in 1968, three weeks before King's assassination. But there was no record of Romney Snr attending, and Romney Jnr himself was out of the country at the time. When challenged in December 2007, Romney acknowledged he was 'speaking figuratively'

It's not worth moving heaven and earth spending billions of dollars just trying to catch one person.

ROMNEY, campaign trail, promising that a Romney Presidency would cease the focus on capturing Osama Bin Laden, the Al-Qaeda leader, 26 April 2007

He's going to pay, and he will die.

ROMNEY, presidential debate a week later, signaling what a Romney presidency would do about bin Laden, 3 May 2007

My life experience convinced me that Ronald Reagan was right.

ROMNEY on his Republican credentials, presidential primary campaign, January 2007

I was an independent during the time of Reagan–Bush; I'm not trying to return to Reagan–Bush.

ROMNEY, during his campaign for the Senate, 1994

Index

Index

Index

Index

Index

Index

Index

Index

Index

Index

Index